ENABLED *by the* POWER OF CHRIST

Enabled *by the* Power of Christ

E. Richard Packham

CFI
Springville, Utah

ISBN 13: 978-1-59955-227-9

Published by CFI, an imprint of Cedar Fort, Inc., 2373 W. 700 S., Springville, UT 84663
Distributed by Cedar Fort, Inc. www.cedarfort.com

LIBRARY OF CONGRESS CATALOGING-IN-PUBLICATION DATA

Packham, E. Richard
Enabled by the Power of Christ / E. Richard Packham.
p. cm.
ISBN 978-1-59955-227-9 (alk. paper)
1. Title

BX8643.J4 P33 2009
dc 232/.3 22

2008041487

Cover design by Angela D. Olsen
Cover design © 2008 by Lyle Mortimer
Edited and typeset by Melissa J. Caldwell

Printed in the United States of America

10 9 8 7 6 5 4 3 2 1

Printed on acid-free paper

Other Books by E. Richard Packham

Born of the Spirit

Contents

Preface

How easy it is for some to feel that it is beyond their ability to live the life outlined by the gospel of the Lord Jesus Christ. They feel that, for some reason, they are just not cut out to become celestial and fit more easily into terrestrial or telestial molds. My wife and I are close to a young man who, with a good deal of effort, prepared himself for a successful mission during which he baptized over a hundred people. His mission president said that he was one of the best missionaries he had in his mission. Yet, not long after returning, the pull of his former life seemed to draw him away from that which he experienced in the mission field. As parents attempted to counsel and even plead with him to remember and return to that which he was giving up, his response almost always was, "Some of us just aren't cut out to be celestial." That comment implies his belief that there are men and women on earth who do not have the capability to live the type of life necessary to achieve those blessings the Savior promised the faithful.

I have often pondered the dilemma parents face with some children. They ask, "Where did we fail? What else could we have done?" The words the Father spoke to Adam and Eve in the Garden of Eden frequently came to mind: "Nevertheless, thou mayest choose for thyself, for it is given unto thee." Agency is there for all mankind. But, is it true that there are some who just are not *able* to live the principles of the gospel? I believe with all my heart that all of Father's children (excepting those who are not accountable) are able to live the principles taught by the Savior and His prophets. If there were those "not able," would they not have lost agency to choose? If we were to change the words from "unable" to "unwilling," we can easily agree that many, if not most, do not meet celestial standards as we observe the condition of the world about us. But I cannot agree that there are any who are "unable." Those who make such a claim do not understand the power of the key elements of Christ's Atonement and the principles He taught to enable us. It is Satan's influence that convinces some that they are "just not cut out to obtain eternal life."

Those who believe they are unable to live their lives in accordance with the gospel of Jesus Christ do not fully understand the enabling powers that flow from Christ and the principles He taught. We must first realize the consequences of the Fall of mankind and the need for the Atonement of Jesus Christ that enable us to live the type of life required by the gospel. Because of the Fall, we can easily see that no mortal could become celestially qualified without help. There was one exception: Father's Only Begotten Son. Those who have been persuaded by the powers of darkness to believe that somehow they were cut out of a different mold simply do not comprehend the enabling power. The life He lived, the principles He taught, and the powers He makes available to us make it possible for all men to ultimately become celestial in nature. On his own, man cannot do it. The best any of us can do without help is rise to a terrestrial level, or as defined by the Savior, the "good men of the earth." I repeat, *with the help of the Savior's Atonement and the enabling powers within the gospel, every accountable person has the ability to live a life worthy of celestial glory.* They also have the agency to choose not to do so. Those who are without accountability are saved through Christ's Atonement.

The whole purpose of this book is to lay out the empowering principles provided by the Savior that help us overcome the "natural man" and the "carnality of man" to become "a saint through the Atonement of Christ" (Mosiah 3:19; Mosiah 16:3). The road is not easy but within the ability of us all, and certainly worth the effort if we choose to follow the "path," cling to the "iron rod," and partake of "white and most desirable fruit" of the tree of life that brings great joy and peace to the soul. While the angel defined the glorious tree in Father Lehi's dream as the "love of God," he did not define what the "white" and "precious" fruit of the tree represented. I believe a careful reading of Nephi's account in Chapters 8 and 11 of 1 Nephi indicates that the fruit is the greatest manifestation of the Father's love—the offering of His Only Begotten Son as a redemptive sacrifice to save mankind. Lehi's dream is one of the more powerful invitations to "come unto Christ." To come unto Christ means to come to know Him. Knowing Him is much more than knowing about Him. In really knowing Him, we come to love Him, and loving Him provides one of the most significant powers that enables us to put our lives in harmony with His will.

As I now attempt to present thoughts relating to the power of Christ to change our souls, I need to emphasize that I do not speak for the Church, nor can I give authoritative explanations of doctrine. I neither have the right nor the ability to do so. The thoughts presented are my opinions as I have searched the standard works and the statements of the prophets and apostles in an attempt to provide answers to some who have concluded that they cannot live the teachings of the Savior. Only the scriptures and the Brethren speak with authority. What I have done is assemble various statements from authoritative sources and try to let them speak for themselves. If I err in presenting my understanding of what the scriptures and the Brethren have said, I accept full responsibility. My only desire is to be in harmony with them.

The principles of doctrine incorporated in The Church of Jesus Christ of Latter-day Saints are profoundly beautiful and consistent. They are like a magnificent picture puzzle, where a single piece may be without beauty or clarity. But the more all of the pieces of Father's plan of happiness are fit together, the greater the splendor of the vision that is presented to our minds. It is with hope that the material presented herein will help some fit some of the more important pieces together.

Acknowledgments

This book is dedicated with appreciation to my wife, Beverly; my children, Pamela, Bruce, Paul, Richard, Trent, Jonathan, Bryan, Laura and Mindy; and my thirty-five grandchildren who have influenced my life more than they know.

My deep gratitude is also expressed to the many general authorities, scholars, teachers, and friends who, over my lifetime, have helped me to come to understand in a small measure the power of Christ's mission to empower us to achieve our premortal destiny designed for us by a loving Heavenly Father. I have quoted many of them throughout the pages of this book.

In particular, I would like to express deep gratitude to Elder Jeffrey R. Holland of the Quorum of Twelve for profound insights he shared about the incompressible suffering of the Savior with all CES Teachers at the annual CES Conference in August 2000 and also for his Apostolic blessing upon us. Also to Dr. George W. Pace, a close friend for over fifty years and a retired professor of religion at BYU, for allowing me to share his idea of the parable used in the fourth chapter of this book. Brother Pace developed the parable many years ago for a presentation on the Atonement for a seminary classes in Burley, Idaho. I took the liberty of adding some material to his original idea.

1

The Creation and the Fall of Man

The creation may seem to be a topic out of place in a book relating to the enabling power of the Atonement. However, Elder Bruce R. McConkie made the observation that the three pillars of the gospel are the Creation, the Fall of man, and the Atonement of Jesus Christ. The Creation leads to the Fall of man, which shows the necessity of the Atonement of the Savior. There is a reference I read a number of years ago, relating to the Creation, that gives powerful insight about our Heavenly Father's great concern for His children and the Atonement.

Before sharing this reference, I would like to share an insight about the Creation that ended years of frustration and searching on my part. From the time of my mission, I ran into a scriptural dilemma that bothered me. I could not reconcile the creation accounts in Genesis 1 and Moses 2 with those in Genesis 2 and Moses 3. For over thirty years, time spent in prayerful thought and study did not reconcile the sequence of events as outlined in these chapters. For example, let me briefly outline the creation sequence of events in Moses 2 and 3.

Moses 2 (Similar to Genesis 1)

First Day: The earth was without form and void. Light was created and separated the darkness, which became day and night.

Second Day: The waters were separated from the firmament (the heavens) and from those on the earth.

Third Day: The waters on the earth were gathered together to form dry land and seas. Grass, herbs, and trees were created.

Fourth Day: Lights were placed in the firmament (heavens) to divide the day and night; signs; seasons; days and years. The sun, moon, and stars appear.

Fifth Day: Fish and fowl are created.

Sixth Day: Cattle, creeping things, all of the beasts of the earth, and man (male and female) are created, with Adam and Eve given dominion over every living thing. All living things were commanded to multiply and replenish the earth. It appears that everything ended on the sixth day. The man and woman remain unnamed. There is no mention of the seventh day.

Now, as we look at the next chapter, remember the completion of the physical creation has just preceded it in chapter 2.

Moses 3 (Similar to Genesis 2)

Verse 5: There is not yet man upon the earth. There was no flesh on the earth. In the preceding chapter all living things, including man and woman, had been created.

Verse 7: God formed man from the dust of the ground, breathed life into him so that he became a living soul, *the first flesh on the earth*, the first man also. In Moses 2, animals, fish, and fowl were created before man. In this chapter, Adam was named and became the first flesh on the earth.

Verse 8: The Garden of Eden was planted, including the Tree of Life and the Tree of the Knowledge of Good and Evil, apparently after man was created. No garden was mentioned in chapter 2.

Verse 17: A commandment (apparently given to Adam only for Eve had not yet been created) forbade him to partake of the Tree of the Knowledge of Good and Evil.

Verses 19–20: Every beast of the field and fowl of the air were formed and given life. Adam gave names to the cattle, fowl, and beasts of the field. Adam did not yet have "an help meet." In contrast to Moses 2, Moses 3 states that animals and fowl were formed after Adam, but before Eve.

Verses 21–25: Eve is formed from the rib of Adam and given to

Adam as his companion. Adam and Eve begin their life together in the Garden. Eve appears to be the last of the creations. In Moses 2, Adam and Eve were created together after all other living things.

Do you agree that the accounts found in these chapters seem beyond reconciliation? Then one day at a Sidney B. Sperry Symposium at Brigham Young University, I was in a session being taught by an LDS Institute of Religion faculty member from Oregon (whose name I don't even remember). He gave an explanation that caused everything to fall into place. It was a significant, exhilarating moment of my life. I literally floated home to share the insight with my wife and friends. My dilemma of thirty years had been solved.

The solution was so simple! Yet it showed the impact of careful scriptural study. The insight came from Abraham's account of the creation, about which nothing has been said so far. However, Abraham's creation sequence, which basically coincides with Moses 2, has some significant differences. For one thing, Abraham uses the term *time* rather than *day* to define the events of the creation. This change seems to imply that the time period may not be a twenty-four hour day as we know it; or perhaps not even a one-thousand-year period of the Lord's time. Even though the event sequence is quite similar to Moses 2, another significant difference in Abraham 4 is when living things (plants, animals, and man) are created. The significant change that begins to reconcile the creation accounts in Abraham 4 is that, for living things, the process was only initiated and was not completed as implied in Moses 2 and Genesis 1.

After each event of the creation of living things, the statement is made, "And the Gods saw that they would be obeyed." *Every event* relating to the creation of living things in Abraham 4 was placed in the future tense. The creation was started, but not completed by the conclusion of the sixth day. Listen to the statement that concludes the sixth day in Abraham:

"And the Gods said: We *will do* [future tense] everything that we have said, and organize them; and behold, they *shall be* very obedient.

And it came to pass that it was from evening until morning they called night; and it came to pass that it was from morning until evening that they called day; and they numbered the sixth time" (Abraham 4:31; emphasis added).

At the end of the sixth day, the creation of living things still had not been completed. When were they completed? Listen to what happens on the seventh day in Abraham 5:

> "And thus *we will finish the heavens and the earth, and all the hosts of them.* And the Gods said among themselves: On the seventh time we will end our work, which we have counseled; and we will rest on the seventh time from all our work which we have counseled. . . . And the Gods came down and formed these the generations of the heavens and of the earth, when they were formed in the day that the Gods formed the earth and the heavens, according to all that which they had said concerning *every plant of the field before it was in the earth, and every herb of the field before it grew; for the Gods had not caused it to rain upon the earth when they counseled to do them, and had not formed a man to till the ground.*" (Abraham 5:1–2,4–5; emphasis added)

Could it be that the actual completion of living things on the earth took place after the sixth day; even on the seventh day? Abraham certainly seems to imply that. Even the Doctrine and Covenants sustains that view: "Q. What are we to understand by the sounding of the trumpets, mentioned in the 8th chapter of Revelation? A. We are to understand that as God made the world in six days, and *on the seventh day he finished his work,* and sanctified it, and *also formed man out of the dust of the earth,* even so, in the beginning of the seventh thousand years will the lord God sanctify the earth, and complete the salvation of man" (D&C 77:12; emphasis added).

Does not the Lord say that on the seventh day he finished the work he had begun earlier? The seventh day is truly the day commemorating the time where the Creators finished the work of creation and then started their rest. From these scriptures in Abraham and the Doctrine and Covenants, we can conclude that there are four phases in the creation of things as we know it on earth today.

Spirit Creation. The first phase was the creation of the spirits of all living things, which I will call the Spirit Creation. There is no account given in the standard works of the Spirit Creation. Listen to Elder Joseph Fielding Smith: "The account of the creation of the earth as given in Genesis and the Book of Moses, and as given in the temple, is the creation of the physical earth, and of physical animals and plants. . . . There is no account of the creation of man or other forms of life when they were created as spirits."[1]

Creation of Non-living Things. The accounts of the creation of non-living things, the second phase of the Creation, was started and finished within six days as outlined in Genesis 1, Moses 2, and Abraham 4.

Spiritual Creation of Living Things. The third phase (which coincides with the second phase), the one I had completely overlooked, was a preliminary, spiritual creation of living things, where all living things were started in some way in heaven and called a spiritual creation, and then finished later. This account is also part of Genesis 1, Moses 2 and Abraham 4; and takes place within the six days. In fact the Lord even declares that there was a prior, spiritual creation as we begin the Creation account of the seventh day in Moses 3. Apparently something happened in heaven that was necessary before living things could be physically completed on the earth on the seventh day.

> And I, God, blessed the seventh day, and sanctified it; because that in it I had rested from all my work which I, God, had created and made.
>
> And now, behold, I say unto you, that these are the generations of the heaven and of the earth, when they were created, in the day that I, the Lord God, made the heaven and the earth.
>
> And every plant of the field before it was in the earth, and every herb of the field before it grew. For I, the Lord God, created all things of which I have spoken, spiritually, before they were naturally upon the face of the earth. . . . And I, the Lord God, had created all the children of men; and not yet a man to till the ground; for in heaven created I them; and there was not yet flesh upon the earth, neither in the water, neither in the air. (Moses 3:3–5)

Completion of the Physical Creation of Living Things. The fourth phase was the completion of all living things that were begun in heaven, wherein they were placed physically upon the earth. This account is shown in Genesis 2, Moses 3, and Abraham 5; and takes place on the seventh day. Then the creators sanctified the seventh day and rested from their labors because it was the day their work was completed.

The seminar, where all these things fell into place and solved my personal scriptural dichotomy, was a noteworthy day of my life.

The Garden of Eden

Sometime during the spiritual creation, before Adam and Eve were physically placed on the earth, the Lord told both Adam and Eve (and all of living things) that they were to "be fruitful, and multiply, and replenish the earth" (Moses 2:28). The whole purpose of the Creation, the earth, and everything in it was to provide a place where the Father could send His spirit children (and other living things) away from His presence to obtain a physical body, to have agency to choose between good and evil, to be tested and tried in all things, to learn the lessons of life, to learn how to control their physical passions, and to strive to obtain the qualities and attributes that would ultimately allow them to become like their Heavenly Parents. In order to provide this testing and this opposition, Satan would have to have access to Father's children. Sin, transgression, and disobedience had to be introduced to provide the tests, trials, and opposition. Also, they would have to become mortal in order to provide mortal bodies for Father's spirit children.

After Adam was physically placed on the earth, the Father gave him a commandment, the breaking of which would bring about the purposes for which man was placed on the earth. As outlined in Genesis 2 and Moses 3, the commandment was very specific: "Of every tree of the garden thou mayest freely eat, but of the tree of knowledge of good and evil, thou shalt not eat of it, nevertheless, thou mayest choose for thyself, for it is given unto thee; but, *remember that I forbid it,* for in the day thou eatest thereof thou shalt surely die" (Moses 3:16–17; emphasis added).

Was it necessary for Lucifer to come and tempt Adam and Eve to disobey Father Elohim? Was it necessary for Adam and Eve to partake of the forbidden fruit of the tree of knowledge of good and evil? Absolutely, without question! Are we not told the same things had been done in other prior worlds? Also Father Lehi clearly states that it was necessary:

> And after Adam and Eve had partaken of the forbidden fruit they were driven out of the garden of Eden, to till the earth.
>
> And they have brought forth children; yea, even the family of all the earth.
>
> And the days of the children of men were prolonged, according to the will of God, that they might repent while in the flesh; wherefore, their state became a state of probation, and their time was lengthened, according to the commandments which the Lord God gave unto the children of men. For he gave commandment that all men must repent; for he showed unto all men that they were lost, because of the transgression of their parents.
>
> And now, behold, if Adam had not transgressed he would not have fallen, but he would have remained in the garden of Eden. And all things which were created must have remained in the same state in which they were after they were created; and they must have remained forever, and had no end.
>
> And they would have had no children; wherefore they would have remained in a state of innocence, having no joy, for they knew no misery; doing no good, for they knew no sin.
>
> But behold, all things have been done in the wisdom of him who knoweth all things.
>
> Adam fell that men might be; and men are, that they might have joy." (2 Nephi 2:19–25)

In their innocence in the Garden, before partaking of the forbidden fruit, Adam and Eve *could not* have fulfilled the purpose of the Creation. They would never have had children. All living things, including Adam and Eve, would never have experienced death or decay. Neither would they have produced posterity. There would have been no opposition, no tests, no trials, no adversity, and no misery to teach them and give them spiritual opposition to help them develop the spiritual muscles and qualities of character to become like their Heavenly Parents.

Before partaking of the forbidden fruit, did either Adam or Eve *know* that it was necessary for them to do so? I do not believe so. They knew only that they had been "forbidden" to eat of it. They succumbed to Lucifer and disobeyed Father. Had either of them known that they needed to disobey to fulfill all of the purposes of God in His creation, there would have been no disobedience or transgression. Remember that the Father emphasized in His instruction: "Remember that I forbid it." (Moses 3:17) Also, in Moses 4, when confronted by the Lord after their disobedience, neither of them defended their action with the best answer they could have given: "We were just doing that which was necessary to fulfill the purposes of our creation." Defending what they had done were the first incidents of "passing the buck." Didn't Adam blame Eve and Eve blame the Serpent? (Moses 4:17–19). Even Lucifer had an excuse. However, to Eve's credit, almost immediately after she had partaken of the fruit, she quickly recognized the one who tempted her. She quickly began to recognize the necessity of that which was going to happen to them and that it was a necessary part of Father's plan for them. She used that knowledge to persuade Adam to partake and thus they began the experience of mortality.

Now I will share a historical insight about how Elohim and Jehovah may have felt about the creation of Adam and Eve and the need for the Atonement. The following quote does not have the same validity as the standard works. However, since Elder Russell M. Nelson used this quote in an article for the *Ensign,* it has some basis for its validity. Not only does it show the feelings of the Father and the Son about the creation of man, but also their keen awareness of what would be required of Jehovah in His atoning sacrifice:

> Jesus fulfilled His glorious promise made in pre-earthly councils by atoning for the fall of Adam and Eve unconditionally and for our own sins upon the condition of our repentance. His responsibility as Savior and Redeemer was indelibly intertwined with His responsibility as Creator.
>
> To shed additional light on this relationship, I would like to share a remarkable quotation I found in a rare book in London one day while searching through the library of the British Museum. It was published as a 20th century English translation of an ancient Egyptian text. It

was written by Timothy, Archbishop of Alexandria, who died in AD 385. This record refers to the creation of Adam; the premortal Jesus is speaking as is His Father [Timothy writes first, and then quotes the Father and Jehovah]: "He made Adam according to Our image and likeness, and He left him lying for forty days and forty nights without putting breath into him. And He heaved sighs over him daily, saying, 'If I put breath into this [man], he must suffer many pains.' And I said unto my Father, 'Put breath into him; I will be an advocate for him.' And my Father said unto me, 'If I put breath into him, My beloved Son, Thou will be obliged to go down into the world, and to suffer many pains for him before Thou shall have redeemed him, and made him to come back to his primal state.' And I said unto my Father, 'Put breath into him; I will be his advocate, and I will go down into the world, and will fulfil Thy command.' "[2]

Consequences of the Fall

It is hard for some to comprehend and accept the incomprehensible impact of the simple act of disobedience when Adam and Eve partook of the forbidden fruit. Prior to their disobedience, I am sure that Adam and Eve did not fully comprehend the simple statement, "For in the day that thou eatest thereof thou shalt surely die" (Moses 3:17). When they ate the fruit of the tree of knowledge of good and evil, what impacted the earth and mankind?

The Fall of the Earth. The earth fell from its terrestrial position near Kolob and the throne of God to its telestial position in orbit around the sun of our solar system (Abraham 5:13; see also Brigham Young, *Journal of Discourses,* vol. 1, 143).

Mortal Death. All living things, including Adam, Eve, and their posterity, became mortal—subject to temptation, physical pain, disease, and physical death. At the appointed time, their spirits would leave their physical bodies, causing them to die and decay in the grave. Prior to the Fall, they would have lived forever in their innocent, semimortal state (2 Nephi 2:19–25).

Ability to Procreate. In their mortal condition, all living things were now able to procreate and reproduce "after their own kind." There was no procreation before the fall (2 Nephi 2: 19–25).

Spiritual Death. Due to disobedience and a sinful nature that resulted, mankind became unclean and separated from the direct presence of God and Christ. Thus, spiritual death prevailed upon mankind. After being cast out of the garden, communication with Adam and Eve and their posterity came primarily through the Holy Ghost and angels (D&C 29:40–42).

Carnality of Man. Agency allowed all mankind to become carnal and an enemy to God. Prior to the Fall, Adam and Eve were innocent and not aware of good and evil (Mosiah 3:19, 16:3).

Work. All men had to work for their "bread" by the "sweat of their brow." They had to till the soil, plant, water, and harvest. In the garden, before the Fall, Adam and Eve were provided food without much effort on their part (Moses 4:23–25).

The above consequences were absolutely needed for men and women to learn the lessons necessary for them to become heirs and achieve the glory of their Heavenly Parents. But there were also problems. With death and the loss of their physical body, they could not become like their Heavenly Parents who had glorified, immortal bodies of flesh and bone. Because of agency, "All [except one] have sinned, and come short of the glory of God" (Romans 3:23). Thus, the "second death" prevails upon all men, for we have become unclean and no unclean thing can enter into the presence of God (1 Nephi 10:21, 15:34; Moses 6:57). Also, without "divine assistance," which according to the Bible Dictionary is essentially the definition of grace, the consequences of the Fall would forever keep mankind from reaching their divine potential. That which was necessary also created significant problems that caused the concern of the Father and Jehovah to ponder the work that had to be done to prepare the way for us. Why it was necessary for the Father's Only Begotten Son to suffer will be discussed in depth in a later chapter. To me, that is the profound question.

The Carnality of Man

We do not hear much about the doctrine of the carnality of man or man's fallen nature in our church meetings. We like to focus on positive, pleasant things. However, if we do not understand the impact of the Fall on man's nature, we cannot fully understand the desperate need we all have for an Atonement. President Ezra Taft Benson powerfully made this point: "Just as man does not really desire food until he is hungry, so he does not, desire the salvation of Christ until he knows why he needs Christ. No one adequately knows why he needs Christ until he understands and accepts the doctrine of the Fall and its effect upon mankind."[3]

Why focus on something so negative as the carnality of man? Because of all of the doctrines in the gospel of Jesus Christ, it is the one that best indicates the need for the enabling power within the Atonement of Christ and His gospel. President Benson inmplied this in the previous quote.

King David properly pondered the question: "What is man that thou art mindful of him?" (Psalm 8:4).

If we add a word, we have a similar question that Latter-day Saints have frequently pondered and debated: "What is man's nature?" As we first begin to contemplate in some depth—God, man, and their relationship to each other, it is natural to have our thoughts develop along this line:

- All mankind are the direct offspring of God: His sons, and daughters.
- God is perfect and divine.
- As children of God, we must inherit His divine qualities and goodness.
- Man must then be naturally good. Can anything bad come from God?

Because we are the sons and daughters of Heavenly Parents, there is no question that we have the potential to become heirs. However, the more deeply I studied the previous conclusions, the more I began to realize that my intellectual reasoning of this basic doctrine is not in harmony with the scriptures and statements of the Brethren. For me, a long period of meditation, research, and prayer resulted from trying to harmonize what the prophets have said with what I thought the world to be like. In my adult life, I have had many opportunities to associate with people not of our faith. Most of my non-LDS friends were not bad people. They were basically good people, who tried most of the time to do what they felt was right. Very few of those I associated with were liars, adulterers, thieves, murderers, and so forth. So why is man thought to be carnal?

I will use just a few scriptures from the standard works to show the dilemma I faced. What do the prophets say with regard to man's nature? King Benjamin, in his great sermon from the tower and using words given him by an angel, declared: "For the natural man is an enemy to God, and has been from the fall of Adam, and will be, forever and ever, unless he yields to the enticings of the Holy Spirit, and putteth off the natural man and becometh a Saint through the Atonement of Christ the Lord" (Mosiah 3:19).

What could this great prophet King be saying? How could man be an enemy to God? Listen to Abinadi, the great prophet martyr: "For they are carnal and devilish, and the devil has power over them; yea even that old serpent that did beguile our first parents, which was the cause of their fall; which was the cause of all mankind becoming carnal, sensual, devilish, knowing evil from good, subjecting themselves to the devil" (Mosiah 16:3).

Even that leader of great faith, the Brother of Jared, declares: "O Lord, thou hast said that we must be encompassed about by the floods. Now behold, O Lord, and do not be angry with thy servant because of his weakness before thee; for we know that thou art holy and dwellest in the heavens, and that we are unworthy before thee; *because of the fall our natures have become evil continually*" (Ether 3:2; emphasis added).

Did the Fall of our first parents cause all mankind to become "carnal, sensual, and devilish"? Surely we are not like that! But again we read Alma's counsel to his son Corianton in describing the result of man's carnality: "Therefore, as the soul could never die, and the fall had brought upon all mankind a *spiritual death* as well as a temporal, that is, they were cut off from the presence of the Lord, it was expedient that mankind should be reclaimed from this spiritual death. Therefore, as *they had become carnal, sensual, and devilish, by nature,* this probationary state became a state for them to prepare; it became a preparatory state" (Alma 42:9–10; emphasis added).

Even our modern scriptures agree: "[He] gave unto them commandments that they should love and serve him, the only living and true God, and that he should be the only being whom they should worship. But by the transgression of these holy laws *man became sensual and devilish, and became fallen man*" (D&C 20:19–20; emphasis added. See also Alma 5:22–25; 41:10–14; Moses 5:13, 55; 6:15, 49, 55).

There certainly seems to be a uniformity of opinion among the prophets of old. But how about the prophets of our day? Have they changed the scripture's position on this doctrine? In the interest of brevity I will quote just two statements, one from President David O. McKay and one from President Spencer W. Kimball. A number of other statements of latter-day prophets and apostles could be presented, but President McKay's and President Kimball's are representative. In a letter to his son David, President McKay discusses the nature of man:

> In the beginning, whenever that was, man found himself shut out from God's eternal presence. He remembered little and in time would have remembered nothing of his associations with eternal beings. "In his humiliation his judgment was taken away." (Acts 8:33.) Earth and earthly things were everything to him. When he became hungry, it was the earth that satisfied him; when he became thirsty, it was earthly element that quenched his thirst; when he became cold it was the skins of animals that protected him and kept him warm; or it was the great moving luminary in the sky that shed his genial rays on man's chilly limbs; when he sought comfort in repose, it was from the trees, or from skins of animals, or from vegetation of the earth that gave him a downy bed. In short, the earth became not only man's foster mother, she was to him the source of his very existence. Self-preservation became not only the first law but, I can imagine, the only law he knew. As the race increased, and the struggle for existence became more acute, selfishness and strife would manifest themselves. Man would struggle with man

> for supremacy or for the best things nature could offer for the prolongation or the comforts of life. Thus would man become "carnal, sensual, and devilish" by nature. (Alma 42:6–13.)[4]

President Kimball states in his powerful treatment of sin, repentance, and forgiveness: "In summary, the way to eternal life is clear. It is well marked. It is difficult. Evil and good influences will be ever present. One must choose. Generally the evil way is the easier, and since man is carnal that way will triumph unless there be a conscious and consistently vigorous effort to reject the evil and follow the good."[5]

As I researched the subject, I could find nothing from the standard works that directly stated that man's basic nature after the Fall is good or godlike. The nearest I could find was a statement in the Doctrine and Covenants: "Every spirit of man was innocent in the beginning; and God having redeemed man from the fall, men became again, *in their infant state,* innocent before God" (D&C 93:38; emphasis added).

There are also several other scriptures stating that "little children are alive in Christ." Do these statements contradict those quoted earlier? Obviously the prophets will not contradict themselves and both concepts are harmonious. These scriptures do not define man's nature after arriving at the age of accountability. They tell us merely that when a man is born as a mortal child, he is innocent and free from the bondage of any sin resulting from the disobedience of his parents, the transgression of Adam and Eve, or any innocent act of disobedience committed before knowing the difference between good and evil (see also D&C 29:47; 74:6–7; Moroni 8:8–22; Mosiah 3:16).

Man is free, at the age of accountability, to choose the course his life will take and is under no compulsion from God or any other power to do other than that which he chooses. The Atonement of Christ freely pays the price, penalty, or debt incurred prior to accountability. Again, it is obvious that my initial thoughts with regard to the nature of man were out of harmony with what the prophets have taught.

As I pondered what the prophets had said about our premortal existence, the thought struck me with much force that Lucifer and one-third of our Father's spirit children completely rebelled against our Father, to the point of having to be rejected and cast out. This rebellion was in His presence and with full knowledge of the consequences. This rebellion seems to discount the idea that being the posterity of Heavenly Parents causes us to inherit their nature and qualities of character. Perhaps the ego or intelligence (or the personality part of man), which is coeternal with God, had more to with our character there than did Heavenly Parents providing a spirit body to house the eternal personality. Perhaps our spirit birth to Heavenly parents was not the controlling factor as to the qualities of character we possess, since that part of us is eternal. Our Heavenly Parents' example to their spirit children was perfect and their love without flaw; but their children, including Lucifer, had agency as to whether or not they would follow the perfect examples of their Heavenly Parents. They lost one-third of their spirit children to Lucifer.

Still I was left with the problem of reconciling what the prophets had said about man's nature with the basic goodness I saw in society about me. In preparing a lesson for an early morning seminary class, the solution that finally satisfied my mind came in a sudden burst of insight as I was reading and pondering the fourth chapter of 2 Nephi, also known as the great Psalm of Nephi. Here, Nephi bears his soul:

> Behold, my soul delighteth in the things of the Lord; and my heart pondereth continually upon the things which I have seen and heard.
>
> Nevertheless, notwithstanding the great goodness of the Lord, in showing me his great and marvelous works, my heart exclaimeth:
>
> O wretched man that I am! Yea, my heart sorroweth because of my flesh; my soul grieveth because of mine iniquities.
>
> I am encompassed about, because of the temptations and the sins which do so easily beset me. And when I desire to rejoice, my heart groaneth because of my sins; nevertheless, I know in whom I have trusted. (2 Nephi 4:16–19)

Here is a prophet who we never read of faltering or wavering in his faith. Even when Father Lehi momentarily lost faith, Nephi didn't. He had beheld the Lord and had also beheld things "too great for man."

Even in the greatest of adverse circumstances, Nephi's faith prevailed and persevered. How could Nephi say these things about himself in verses 17–19? Was Nephi a wicked person? No! In the eyes of his associates he would have been considered the most righteous of men. The light dawned! The prophets, being as close to Christ as they are, have a different standard of measurement of goodness than we do! Their standard of righteousness is that of a Christlike life, a life that holds nothing back with respect to time, talent, energy, and means in the service of God; a life reflective of Father Abraham's submissiveness to sacrifice his most precious possession, his son, Isaac. Now, if this is the scriptural standard for good, how many men are good? Indeed are we not all enemies to God unless we "putteth off the natural man and becometh a saint through the Atonement of Christ" (Mosiah 3:19)? The prophets are not trying to tell us that all men are evil according to our standard of measurement, but that they have a long way to go with respect to being Christlike.

In other words, men are selfish. The "natural man" would rather do what he wants rather than what God wants. Many people go to church for an hour on Sunday. But how many of our neighbors would be willing to give a tithe of their time or more to the Lord? Aren't baseball, movies, television, boating, and skiing more important than keeping the Sabbath day holy? How many men will give 10 percent, 15 percent, 20 percent, or all they have to the Lord? Or are new cars, lovely homes, and summer cottages more important?

How about members of the Church? Do we have elements of carnality in us? The law of tithing has been strongly taught as a commandment since 1831. It is even a schoolmaster law (a lesser law) to bring us to the higher law of consecration. Yet what percentage of the Church keeps this commandment: 100 percent? Since 1831, the Lord has said He desired members to attend sacrament meeting. Certainly a simple request like this, requiring only about one and a half hours of our time, is kept 100 percent. Only very recently the Lord, through his prophet, commanded us to have family home evening once a week for the preservation of our families. Surely more would respond to such an important need, at such a small price. How many LDS families are faithful in this request? The Brethren continually advise us not to watch R-rated moves, read books or magazines that focus on sex and immorality, or watch soap opera that have the same focus. In these cases are not many Church members saying, "What I want to do is more important than what God wants me to do"? If we do so, are we then not "carnal, sensual, and devilish" by giving in to the earthly desires—seeking pleasure, ease, carnal desires, and no responsibility—rather than obeying the counsels of the Lord through His servants?

One could get the impression from the scriptures dealing with the nature of man that there are but two levels of righteousness—the "evil" level and the "Christlike life" level. I don't believe that this conclusion is consistent with sections 76 and 131 of the Doctrine and Covenants. The prophets have not stated that there could not be varying degrees of carnality. To be consistent with section 76, we have to conclude that there are at least terrestrial carnality, telestial carnality, and son of perdition carnality. Obviously those striving for a Christlike life would qualify for exaltation in the celestial kingdom. According to section 131 of the Doctrine and Covenants, there are two lower levels in the celestial kingdom; thus, I have to conclude that there are varying degrees of obedience to qualify for lower degrees in the celestial kingdom.

Of what value is the knowing of the carnality of man? Is it important to our exaltation? Without the understanding of our own condition in relationship to prophet's standard of righteousness, we can become very complacent. If Nephi of old has the perspective of his own worthiness before the Lord as he declares in 2 Nephi 4:16–19, then how much more do we need to be concerned of our condition? Knowing, as Nephi knew, of our own need draws us to our only source of relief: Jesus Christ and His sacrifice. The more we know Him, the greater our love for Him and the greater power we have to emulate His life and partake of His sacrifice that can cleanse, sanctify, and empower.

At the times in my life when I have become complacent—feeling I have it made because I pay my tithes and offerings, obey the Word of Wisdom, attend my Church meetings, and render Church service—Nephi's perspective of a Christlike life returns to humble me. We cannot become as the Pharisees of old and feel that because we are good, according to the world's standard of measurement, we have no further room for improvement. Until we strive to become Christlike through His Atonement and consecrate our best effort to doing the Father's will, we cannot rest with an attitude of complacency.

The Prophet's Standard of Righteousness

It is important that we reflect more deeply about the standard of a Christlike life, used by the prophets as a frame of reference for goodness. The man Jesus Christ was born of a mortal mother and immortal Father approximately two thousand years ago. He was a spiritual giant beyond examination. Of all who have ever lived or will yet live on this earth, there are none to compare with His intellectual genius. Likewise no one will ever compare with His unfathomable wisdom or with His spiritual strength and powers. No one will ever be closer to the Father in unity, thought, determination, and action. If any man had the ability to determine his own course or to say "I did it my way," it was Christ the Lord. His combination of intellectual and spiritual capacity would have given Him that ability. Notwithstanding His great wisdom and ability, and here is the key to Christlike life, Jesus states:

> Verily, verily, I say unto you, the Son can do nothing of himself, but what he seeth the Father do: for what things so ever he doeth, these also doeth the Son likewise. (John 5:19)

> For I came down from heaven, not to do mine own will, but the will of him that sent me. (John 6:38)

> I speak not of myself: but the Father that dwelleth in me, he doeth the works. (John 14:10)

Even with the great ability He had, Jesus did nothing of Himself.

His whole effort was totally submissive to the Father's will. All that He did, all that He spoke, was given of the Father. If Jesus found it necessary to draw His course of action from God, then we have a greater need to be dependent upon the Father to determine the course of our lives in every detail. Those who would follow Christ cannot subscribe to "I did it my way," but must strive to emulate the Savior by eliminating those things in their lives that are not Christlike.

The Effects of Sin

The human soul is like a sponge. It absorbs that to which it is exposed. It is a composite of all our acts, thoughts, and experiences. If we expose ourselves to the good, the virtuous, the uplifting, it becomes a part of us, and our decisions and actions reflect those things we have absorbed. In contrast when we participate in evil acts, see X- or R-rated movies, read filthy novels or magazines, associate with bad companions, think evil thoughts, lie, cheat, or steal, these also become a part of us just like dirty water becomes part of a sponge. The Book of Mormon prophets liken such a condition to becoming filthy or unclean:

> Wherefore, if ye have sought to do wickedly in the days of your probation, then ye are found unclean before the judgment-seat of God; and no unclean thing can dwell with God; wherefore, ye must be cast off forever. (1 Nephi 10:21)
>
> And I say unto you again that he cannot save them in their sins; for I cannot deny his word, and he hath said that no unclean thing can inherit the kingdom of heaven; therefore, how can ye be saved, except ye inherit the kingdom of heaven? Therefore, ye cannot be saved in your sins. (Alma 11:37)
>
> And he doth not dwell in unholy temples; neither can filthiness or anything which is unclean be received into the kingdom of God; therefore I say unto you the time shall come, yea, and it shall be at the last day, that he who is filthy shall remain in his filthiness. (Alma 7:21)

Is it a stretch of reason to compare the human soul to a sponge? In a BYU-Idaho Education Week talk on resurrection given in May 2003, Brother Philip Allred of the BYU-Idaho Religion Faculty makes a powerful case that every act and thought of our lives are literally recorded in the fibers, tissues, nerves, and spirit of our body. He shows that this recording on our bodies will rise with us if our bodies have not had the sanctifying renewal of the resurrection, where our bodies will be in a sanctified, glorified condition, and all that is bad will have been erased. Just one quote of the many Brother Allred provided will be used: "Every thought, word and deed has an effect on the human body; all these leave their marks. . . . The Great Judge will then read the record of the book of their lives; the account of their obedience or disobedience will be written on their bodies."[6]

When we cease the act of sinning, we merely stop pouring the dirty water over the sponge. Stopping the addition of new stains does not automatically remove the old, and we are left with the problems of the past. President Joseph F. Smith explains this concept like this: "Men cannot forgive their own sins; they cannot cleanse themselves from the consequences of their sins. Men can stop sinning and can do the right in the future, and so far their acts are acceptable before the Lord and worthy of consideration. But who shall repair the wrongs they have done to themselves and to others, which it seems impossible for them to repair themselves."[7]

What is there to eliminate the accumulation of years of stain? Is the carnal man without hope? What is there in the gospel plan to wring out the sponge of our souls so that we can become sufficiently clean and pure to return to Father's presence? From whence does the spiritual power come?

Notes

1. Joseph Fielding Smith, *Doctrines of Salvation,* vol. 1 (Salt Lake City: Bookcraft, 1954), 75–76.
2. "Discourse on Abbaton by Timothy, Archbishop of Alexandria," *Coptic Martyrdoms etc. in the Dialect of Upper Egypt*, ed. and trans., E. A. Wallis Budge, 1977, as quoted in Russell M. Nelson, "Jesus the Christ: Our Master and More," *Ensign*, Apr. 2000, 13.
3. Ezra Taft Benson, *Ensign*, June 1992, 7.
4. David O. McKay, quoted in *Instructor,* Mar. 1959, 65–66.

5. Spencer W. Kimball, *The Miracle of Forgiveness* (Salt Lake City: Bookcraft, 1969), 15.
6. Bruce R. McConkie, *Mormon Doctrine* (Salt Lake City: Bookcraft, 1958), 97, as quoted by Philip Allred at a BYU-Idaho Education Week, May 2003.
7. Joseph F. Smith, *Gospel Doctrine* (Salt Lake City: Deseret Book, 1977), 98–99.

2

The Enabling Power of the Atonement of Jesus Christ

As members of the Church complete their study of the four gospels, they briefly walk in the footsteps of the Savior as He taught the multitudes, established His earthly kingdom, healed the sick, raised the dead, and calmed the elements. Finally, they spend a few sacred hours with Him in a lonely garden called Gethsemane and on a barren hill called Golgotha. Perhaps tears may fill their eyes as they ponder the significance of these final hours of the Master's mortal life and wonder at the love that compelled Him to submit willingly to the events that produced blood from the pores of His body and caused nails to tear His flesh.

No one can fully comprehend the significance of the Savior's Atonement as it relates to themselves as an individual. Sometimes we find it difficult to understand how the sacrificial suffering of one individual two thousand years ago can cleanse us of sin and remove the sting of death. The question may also come to mind as to why a kind and loving Heavenly Father, who has all power and all knowledge, would cause His Only Begotten Son to suffer, as was required of Jesus. Why not some other way? The lack of adequate answers to these and other deep questions cause in some a feeling of uneasiness or discomfort; thus, some avoid, or fear, the effort necessary to understand their relationship to the Atonement of the Holy Messiah. The lack of answers to some of these questions has even caused some to falter and some to reject the doctrine of a suffering Redeemer, which rejection, according to the prophets, causes them to become infidel.

As Church members embark on the study of the Book of Mormon, the sacred scriptures therein offer insight to help them understand the difficult questions about our Savior's sacrifice. We cannot approach this doctrine without a feeling of awe and inadequacy. We will never fully comprehend its scope and magnitude as long as we are limited by the veil of mortality. However, the apostles, prophets, and the quiet whisperings of the Holy Spirit point the way so we can understand sufficiently to personally partake of the offering made by Christ on our behalf. A significant benefit flowing into our beings as we come to have a deeper understanding of the Savior's Atonement will be the realization of the majestic enabling power of His sacrifice.

The Doctrinal Position of the Atonement

Not all doctrines and commandments are of equal importance. What is the position of the Atonement of the Savior as a point of doctrine? A series of questions, rhetorically presented by Joseph Smith, stated the position of the Church on many issues. One question he asked was, "What is the fundamental principle of your religion?" His answer was succinct and profound: "The fundamental principles of our religion are the testimony of the Apostles and Prophets, concerning Jesus Christ, that he died, was buried, and rose again the third day and ascended into heaven; and *all other things which pertain to our religion are only appendages to it.*"[1]

James E. Talmage writes about the consequence of rejecting the Atonement: "However incomplete may be our comprehension of the scheme of the redemption through Christ's vicarious sacrifice in all of its parts, *we cannot reject it without becoming infidel,* for it stands as the fundamental doctrine of all scripture, the very essence of the spirit of prophesy and revelation; the most prominent of all of the declarations of God unto man."[2]

Jacob also testifies that the central focus of all scripture is the Atonement of the Savior as Jacob testifies: "Behold my soul delighteth in proving unto my people the truth of the coming of Christ; for, for this end hath the law of Moses been given; and *all things which have been given of God from the beginning of the world unto now are the typifying of him*" (2 Nephi 11:4; emphasis added).

One final witness from Elder Boyd K. Packer:

> "For there is one God, and one mediator between God and men, the man Christ Jesus" (1 Timothy 2:5). Through him mercy can be fully extended to each of us without offending the eternal law of justice.
>
> This truth is the very root of Christian doctrine. You may know much about the gospel as it branches out from there; but if you only know the branches and those branches do not touch the root, if they have been cut from that truth, there will be no life nor substance nor redemption in them.[3]

A knowledge of the importance of Christ's sacrifice, in and of itself, does not necessarily help us to understand some of the deep questions relating to the doctrine. However, it is a significant beginning, for as we understand its importance and begin to ponder the questions, we open our hearts to the power of the Spirit. One can never come to terms with the Atonement on the basis of intellect alone. Only as the Spirit speaks to spirit will a person's soul be satisfied and committed and sanctified.

A Suffering Redeemer

Both ancient and modern prophets relate a very powerful awareness of the depth of the sacrifice that was made by Christ, our Savior. It is not a pleasant experience to contemplate the suffering endured by the Savior, particularly as we realize that the crushing weight of our personal sins contribute to that suffering. To approach it, even in our thoughts, is to come onto holy ground. As Moses was commanded, perhaps we should "put off [our] shoes from off [our] feet for the place whereon [we] standest is holy ground," as we approach this subject. We sometimes hesitate to think of Christ's sacrifice for us. However, the prophets place sufficient emphasis upon it that it must be important for us to understand. Just a few of many references will be used to give the perspective of the prophets regarding this sacred theme.

Book of Mormon Prophets Testify. Book of Mormon prophets had a deep knowledge of Christ's suffering revealed to them. Read the words of Jacob and King Benjamin as representative of Book of Mormon prophets:

> O how great the holiness of our God; for he knoweth all things, and there is not anything save he knows it.
>
> And he cometh into the world that he may save all men if they will hearken unto his voice; for behold, he suffereth the pains of all men, yea, the pains of every living creature, both men, women, and children, who belong to the family of Adam. (2 Nephi 9:20–21)

> And the things which I shall tell you are made known unto me by an angel from God. And he said unto me. . . .
>
> For behold, the time cometh, and is not far distant, that with power, the Lord Omnipotent who reigneth, who was, and is from all eternity to all eternity, shall come down from heaven among the children of men, and shall dwell in a tabernacle of clay, and shall go forth amongst men, working mighty miracles, such as healing the sick, raising the dead, causing the lame to walk, the blind to receive their sight, and the deaf to hear, and curing all manner of diseases. . . .
>
> And lo, he shall suffer temptations, and pain of body, hunger, thirst, and fatigue, even more than man can suffer, except it be unto death; for behold, blood cometh from every pore, so great shall be his anguish for the wickedness and the abominations of his people. (Mosiah 3:2, 5, 7)

(For further information, see also Mosiah 14:1–12; 15:7-12; Alma 7:11–14; 22:14–15; 34:8–17; 42:13–17; 3 Nephi 27:13–15, 19–21.)

Modern Apostles and Prophets' Testimonies. President Joseph Fielding Smith relates the following with regard to the suffering of the Savior:

> A great many people have an idea that when he was on the cross, and nails were driven into his hands and feet, that was his great suffering. His great suffering was before he ever was placed upon the cross. It was in the Garden of Gethsemane that the blood oozed from the pores of his body: "Which suffering caused myself, even God, the greatest of all, to tremble because of pain, and to bleed at every pore, and to suffer both body and spirit—and would that I might not drink the bitter cup, and shrink."

That was not when he was on the cross; that was in the garden. That is where he bled from every pore in his body.

Now I cannot comprehend that pain. I have suffered pain, you have suffered pain and sometimes it has been quite severe; but I cannot comprehend pain, which is mental anguish more than physical, that would cause blood, like sweat, to come out upon the body. It was something terrible, something terrific; so we can understand why he would cry unto his Father, "If it be possible, let this cup pass from me: nevertheless not as I will, but as thou wilt."[4]

The Savior revealed to Joseph Smith the depth of his suffering:

For behold, I, God, have suffered these things for all, that they might not suffer if they would repent; but if they would not repent they must suffer even as I;

Which suffering caused myself, even God, the greatest of all, to tremble because of pain, and to bleed at every pore, and to suffer both body and spirit—and would that I might not drink the bitter cup, and shrink—

Nevertheless, glory be to the Father, and I partook and finished my preparations unto the children of men. (D&C 19:16–19)

The testimony of James E. Talmage follows:

Christ's agony in the garden is unfathomable by the finite mind, both as to intensity and cause. The thought that He suffered through fear of death is untenable. Death to Him was preliminary to resurrection and triumphal return to the Father from whom He had come, and to a state of glory even beyond what He had before possessed; and, moreover, it was within His power to lay down His life voluntarily. He struggled and groaned under a burden such as no other being who has lived on earth might even conceive as possible. It was not physical pain, nor mental anguish alone, that caused Him to suffer such torture as to produce an extrusion of blood from every pore; but a spiritual agony of soul such as only God was capable of experiencing. No other man, however great his powers of physical or mental endurance, could have suffered so; for his human organism would have succumbed, and syncope would have produced unconsciousness and welcome oblivion. In that hour of anguish Christ met and overcame all the horrors that Satan, "the prince of this world" could inflict. The frightful struggle incident to the temptations immediately following the Lord's baptism was surpassed and overshadowed by this supreme contest with the powers of evil.

At the ninth hour, or about three in the afternoon, a loud voice, surpassing the most anguished cry of physical suffering issued from the central cross, rending the dreadful darkness. It was the voice of the Christ: "Eloi, Eloi, lama sabachthani?" which being interpreted, "My God, my God, why hast thou forsaken me?" What mind of man can fathom the significance of that awful cry? It seems, that in addition to the fearful suffering incident to crucifixion, the agony of Gethsemane had recurred, intensified beyond human power to endure. In that bitterest hour the dying Christ was alone, alone in the most terrible reality. That the supreme sacrifice of the Son might be consummated in all its fullness, the Father seems to have withdrawn the support of His immediate presence, leaving to the Savior of men the glory of complete victory over the forces of sin and death.

If the soldier's spear was thrust into the left side of the Lord's body and actually penetrated the heart, the outrush of "blood and water" observed by John is further evidence of a cardiac rupture; for it is known that in the rare instances of death resulting from a breaking of any part of the wall of the heart, blood accumulates within the pericardium, and there undergoes a change by which the corpuscles separate as a partially clotted mass from the almost colorless, watery serum.

The present writer believes that the Lord Jesus died of a broken heart. The psalmist sang in dolorous measure according to his inspired prevision of the Lord's passion: "Reproach hath broken my heart; and I am full of heaviness; and I looked for some to take pity, but there was none; and for comforters, but I found none."[5]

New Testament Witnesses. The authors of the four gospels provide significant insight into the degree of the suffering of the Savior. It is interesting that the last week of the Savior's mortal life constitutes about one-third of the total content of the four gospels. I will quote some of the significant scriptures from these chroniclers relating to the suffering of the Savior in Gethsemane and Golgotha. The hour had come, which began in a garden and ended on a hilltop. These events began that which had been anticipated at the time Elohim and Jehovah had pondered the placing of life in the man Adam. They were symbolized in the ordinances of animal sacrifices given to Adam and Eve as they left the Garden of Eden and perpetuated by the prophets from Adam's time to this scene that began in a lonely garden called Gethsemane.

No artist, no matter their talent, could depict the agony of mind, body, and spirit of these events. Even the beautiful picture typically displayed in LDS chapels, showing the Savior in Gethsemane kneeling by a gnarled tree trunk with a mournful look on His face, does not portray the reality of His experience and certainly is not consistent with what the four gospels reveal. Read their words:

Matthew (Matthew 26:36–45)

> 36 Then cometh Jesus with them unto a place called Gethsemane, and saith unto the disciples, Sit ye here, while I go and pray yonder.
>
> 37 And he took with him Peter and the two sons of Zebedee, and began to be sorrowful and very heavy.
>
> 38 Then saith he unto them, My soul is exceeding sorrowful, even unto death: tarry ye here, and watch with me.
>
> 39 And he went a little further, and fell on his face, and prayed, saying, O my Father, if it be possible, let this cup pass from me: nevertheless not as I will, but as thou wilt.

How could an artist portray such pain and agony that threatens to take life? He who had "life in himself," even the ability to keep body and spirit together until He chose to let death end the suffering, struggled to keep body and spirit together. He was not kneeling by a tree trunk with a mournful look on His face, as some pictures depict Him. His agony was such that He literally fell prostate on the ground (Mark 14:35; Matthew 26:39). He has already agreed in His premortal state to undergo this experience, but it became such that even He prayed for it to be removed. Matthew continues:

> 40 And he cometh unto the disciples, and findeth them asleep, and saith unto Peter, What, could ye not watch with me one hour?
>
> 41 Watch and pray, that ye enter not into temptation: the spirit indeed is willing, but the flesh is weak.
>
> 42 He went away again the second time, and prayed, saying, O my Father, if this cup may not pass away from me, except I drink it, thy will be done.
>
> 43 And he came and found them asleep again: for their eyes were heavy.

44 And he left them, and went away again, and prayed the third time, saying the same words.

45 Then cometh he to his disciples, and saith unto them, Sleep on now, and take your rest: behold, the hour is at hand, and the Son of man is betrayed into the hands of sinners.

Three separate times Jesus came to the three sleeping apostles for comfort, the first time after spending an hour in his infinite atoning effort. Could this indicate that it may have been at least three hours of agony beyond what any human could imagine. Three times He asked that if it were possible the cup be taken away, for it almost impossible for even Him to bear. Three times the Father said, "No, it has to be."

Mark (Mark 14:32–42)

32 And they came to a place which was named Gethsemane: and he saith to his disciples, Sit ye here, while I shall pray.

33 And he taketh with him Peter and James and John, and began to be sore amazed, and to be very heavy;

34 And saith unto them, My soul is exceeding sorrowful unto death: tarry ye here, and watch.

35 And he went forward a little, and fell on the ground, and prayed that, if it were possible, the hour might pass from him.

Mark confirms again the location of the beginning of Christ's suffering was Gethsemane. John confirms that after the last supper, Jesus took the eleven Apostles to a garden. It was a place that Jesus loved to visit and in which He frequently visited when in Jerusalem. That is how Judas knew where to find Jesus after leaving the upper room within the walls of Jerusalem. By crossing the brook Cedron, they had to leave the walled city to the east of the temple which led to the Mount of Olives.

According to Elder Jeffrey R. Holland at the annual 2000–2001 CES Conference my wife and I attended, the garden, which was called Gethsemane, also had significance. The literal translation from the Greek comes from *geth,* which means "press," and *seman,* which means "oil." The name *Gethsemane* literally means "oil press." The garden on the Mount of Olives was a garden of olive trees. Even today there are still remnants of ancient olive presses used to make olive oil. Olives are placed in the olive presses and with a screw placed under great pressure that forces the oil to ooze out of the cells of the olive. How significant is the symbolism of an olive press as it relates to what was to occur there. Is it not profound symbolism that the Savior's sacrifice for sin, took place in an olive grove with olive presses nearby. It was not by coincidence. The press became so great that He exclaimed to be "very heavy," even "unto death." The great Jehovah, who had created worlds without out number, knew from the foundation of the world what was going to be required of Him. Christ knew it would test him to the ultimate limit of His Godhood. Even with this foreknowledge, verse 33 in Mark 14 chapter first tells us that what began to happen caused, even Him, the Savior to be "sore amazed."

Elder Holland also stated that a more accurate translation of the Greek term, "sore amazed," would be "terrified surprise." Even the Savior, with His premortal knowledge of the suffering He must endure to pay the price of the sins of all men, was terrified and surprised at the intensity of the pain and agony of spirit. Mark continues:

> 36 And he said, Abba, Father, all things are possible unto thee; take away this cup from me: nevertheless not what I will, but what thou wilt.
>
> 37 And he cometh, and findeth them sleeping, and saith unto Peter, Simon, sleepest thou? couldest not thou watch one hour?
>
> 38 Watch ye and pray, lest ye enter into temptation. The spirit truly is ready, but the flesh is weak.
>
> 39 And again he went away, and prayed, and spake the same words.
>
> 40 And when he returned, he found them asleep again, (for their eyes were heavy,) neither wist they what to answer him.
>
> 41 And he cometh the third time, and saith unto them, Sleep on now, and take your rest: it is enough, the hour is come; behold, the Son of man is betrayed into the hands of sinners.
>
> 42 Rise up, let us go; lo, he that betrayeth me is at hand.

"Abba, Father," according to Elder Holland , was a very personal plea that could be interpreted "Papa or Daddy."

Luke (Luke 22:39–46)

39 And he came out, and went, as he was wont, to the mount of Olives; and his disciples also followed him.

40 And when he was at the place, he said unto them, Pray that ye enter not into temptation.

41 And he was withdrawn from them about a stone's cast, and kneeled down, and prayed,

42 Saying, Father, if thou be willing, remove this cup from me: nevertheless not my will, but thine, be done.

43 And there appeared an angel unto him from heaven, strengthening him.

44 And being in an agony he prayed more earnestly: and his sweat was as it were great drops of blood falling down to the ground.

45 And when he rose up from prayer, and was come to his disciples, he found them sleeping for sorrow,

46 And said unto them, Why sleep ye? rise and pray, lest ye enter into temptation.

Luke adds additional facts not disclosed by Matthew or Mark. The Savior's suffering and closeness to death was such that it was necessary to send an angel from heaven to strengthen Him. It is here also that Luke, along with Book of Mormon prophets, indicates that the intensity of Christ's suffering caused "great drops of blood" to come from the pores of His body. The pressure of the press of the weight of infinite sins, illnesses, and infirmities became so great the corpuscles within His body broke down and began to ooze blood with the sweat of His body. According to medical doctors there is a medical condition called Hematridosis, or a bloody sweat.

John the Beloved (John 18:1–2)

1 When Jesus had spoken these words, he went forth with his disciples over the brook Cedron, where was a garden, into the which he entered, and his disciples.

2 And Judas also, which betrayed him, knew the place: for Jesus ofttimes resorted thither with his disciples.

Gethsemane did not end the suffering. It was only the beginning. There was no time for His body, mind, and spirit to recoup. The betrayal took place almost immediately hereafter. The Savior was taken by the Sanhedrin's soldiers to an illegal midnight trial before Caiaphas, the High Priest, and the Jewish rulers that constituted the Sanhedrin. Here there was no defense attorney to assure His rights were protected. Here witnesses were sought to give false testimony that He might be condemned to death. Here He was ridiculed, berated and struck by the ruler's guards. Here they "spit in His face, buffeted Him, and others smote Him with their hands," (Matthew 26:67) Thus, the long night faded into dawn. A sentence of death was pronounced, which required approval of Roman authority. He was taken before Pilate, who unsuccessfully attempted to have Him freed. Even Pilate knew Jesus was not worthy of death. But the Jewish mobs demanded that He be crucified. Pilate, who had total authority and Roman soldiers to back him up, caved to their wishes. He had Jesus scourged (Matthew 27:26) and then ordered His crucifixion.

Matthew/Mark (Matthew 27:26–35, 39–51; Mark 15:25)

> 26 Then released he Barabbas unto them: and when he had scourged Jesus, he delivered him to be crucified.
>
> 27 Then the soldiers of the governor took Jesus into the common hall, and gathered unto him the whole band of soldiers.
>
> 28 And they stripped him, and put on him a scarlet robe.
>
> 29 And when they had platted a crown of thorns, they put it upon his head, and a reed in his right hand: and they bowed the knee before him, and mocked him, saying, Hail, King of the Jews!
>
> 30 And they spit upon him, and took the reed, and smote him on the head.
>
> 31 And after that they had mocked him, they took the robe off from him, and put his own raiment on him, and led him away to crucify him.
>
> 32 And as they came out, they found a man of Cyrene, Simon by name: him they compelled to bear his cross.

Some have wondered that Jesus, who was about six feet tall and well built, could not carry His own crossbeam up to Golgotha. They do not remember the intense agony, nigh unto death, of several hours duration in Gethsemane that robbed Him of physical and emotional strength. Then, He suffered the Roman ritual scourging from a whip with long leather straps, imbedded with shards of bone and metal. The Roman soldier applied the whip full strength against the bare skin of both the front and back of the victim. Many succumbed to death, just from the scourging. These two events left the Savior without the physical strength to carry the crossbeam to the place of crucifixion.

> 33 And when they were come unto a place called Golgotha, that is to say, a place of a skull,
>
> 34 They gave him vinegar to drink mingled with gall: and when he had tasted thereof, he would not drink.
>
> 35 And they crucified him, and parted his garments, casting lots: that it might be fulfilled which was spoken by the prophet, They parted my garments among them, and upon my vesture did they cast lots. . . .
> [25. And it was the third hour, and they crucified him. (Mark 15:25)]
>
> 39 And they that passed by reviled him, wagging their heads,
>
> 40 And saying, Thou that destroyest the temple, and buildest it in three days, save thyself. If thou be the Son of God, come down from the cross.
>
> 41 Likewise also the chief priests mocking him, with the scribes and elders, said,
>
> 42 He saved others; himself he cannot save. If he be the King of Israel, let him now come down from the cross, and we will believe him.
>
> 43 He trusted in God; let him deliver him now, if he will have him: for he said, I am the Son of God.
>
> 44 The thieves also, which were crucified with him, cast the same in his teeth.
>
> 45 Now from the sixth hour there was darkness over all the land unto the ninth hour.
>
> 46 And about the ninth hour Jesus cried with a loud voice, saying, Eli, Eli, lama sabachthani? that is to say, My God, my God, why hast thou forsaken me?

Elder Melvin J. Ballard of the Quorum of the Twelve proposed in a MIA June Conference message that perhaps at the time Jesus felt forsaken, "[The Father] bowed his head, and hid in some part of the universe, his great heart almost breaking for the love he had for his Son."[6] Something additional happened on the cross at this time that is generally not known. In the ninth hour, after hanging on the cross for approximately six hours, Jesus cries in a loud voice, "My God, my God, why has thou forsaken me?" (Matthew 27:46). Elder James E. Talmage suggests that at this time, in addition to the terrific, physical pain of the cross, "the agony of Gethsemane" also returned for a final period of ultimate agony of body, mind, and spirit.[7] The Romans were experts in meeting out torture and punishment. Hundreds, if not thousands, had been previously crucified. But this one was different. In Gethsemane the Savior had already endured the agony of body and spirit that no other human being could have endured. Because of the size and weight of His body, five large nails or spikes were used—one in each hand, one in each wrist, and one through both feet after the crossbeam had been lifted up to the tree (or post) which were left permanently imbedded in the ground. You have read the account by the Gospel writers. The mind of man cannot comprehend that moment. Matthew continues:

> 47 Some of them that stood there, when they heard that, said, This man calleth for Elias.
>
> 48 And straightway one of them ran, and took a spunge, and filled it with vinegar, and put it on a reed, and gave him to drink.
>
> 49 The rest said, Let be, let us see whether Elias will come to save him.
>
> 50 Jesus, when he had cried again with a loud voice, yielded up the ghost.

In some inexplicable manner, the Savior was able to discern when the last farthing had been paid. He then allowed His spirit to separate from His body into the sweet relief of death. He died of a broken heart.[8] Matthew continues:

> 51 And, behold, the veil of the temple was rent in twain from the top to the bottom; and the earth did quake, and the rocks rent;

John the Beloved (John 19:25–34)

> 25 Now there stood by the cross of Jesus his mother, and his mother's sister, Mary the wife of Cleophas, and Mary Magdalene.
>
> 26 When Jesus therefore saw his mother, and the disciple standing by, whom he loved, he saith unto his mother, Woman, behold thy son!

27 Then saith he to the disciple, Behold thy mother! And from that hour that disciple took her unto his own home.

28 After this, Jesus knowing that all things were now accomplished, that the scripture might be fulfilled, saith, I thirst.

29 Now there was set a vessel full of vinegar: and they filled a spunge with vinegar, and put it upon hyssop, and put it to his mouth.

30 When Jesus therefore had received the vinegar, he said, It is finished: and he bowed his head, and gave up the ghost.

31 The Jews therefore, because it was the preparation, that the bodies should not remain upon the cross on the sabbath day, (for that sabbath day was an high day,) besought Pilate that their legs might be broken, and that they might be taken away.

32 Then came the soldiers, and brake the legs of the first, and of the other which was crucified with him.

33 But when they came to Jesus, and saw that he was dead already, they brake not his legs:

34 But one of the soldiers with a spear pierced his side, and forthwith came there out blood and water.

Elder James E. Talmage has previously indicated that the blood and water that flowed from the Savior's pierced side was indicative that the He had died of a broken heart. When the walls of the heart rupture, the red blood cells coagulate and leave watery serum. Is it not interesting that the actual cause of death of the Savior, a broken heart, is that sacrifice He requires of us to partake of His Atonement and to be born again (2 Nephi 2: 6–7; 3 Nephi 9:20)?

What We Learn From These Testimonies

Much can be learned from those witnesses, who were shown the intensity, width, and depth of the Savior's incomprehensible suffering that goes beyond what any artist can portray with his paints and a brush. Some of the material used in describing the intensity of the suffering of the Savior comes from a magnificent presentation by Elder Jeffrey R. Holland at the conference my wife and I attended as institute and seminary teachers. Elder Holland was the keynote speaker and spoke for about an hour and twenty minutes, introducing the New Testament course of study for the next year. Much of Elder Holland's message focused on the atoning sacrifice of the Savior.

Christ had "life in himself." He had the power to control when He died. During the administration of the sacrament, I have sometimes seen in my mind's eye the suffering He endured. As the press began to bear down upon Christ, He left the presence of Peter, James, and John. He removed His outer robe. Then, as the full weight began to bear down upon Him, in agony He fell upon His face. In my mind's eye, I could see His fingers dig into the cool garden soil of the early April night, fighting to keep body and spirit together until that part of the price was paid. When I felt that I could endure it no more the scene closed.

I believe that Satan was the other party in the garden. He knew if he could win just this battle, he would have won the war. He also threw everything he could muster at the Savior at this most vulnerable time of His life. But Christ won. He did not succumb. He drank the bitter cup to the last drop. The battle fought and won in the garden was the first part of His victory. The agony the Savior experienced was the fierceness of wrath of the Almighty God that will be felt by the wicked who do not repent (Revelation 19:15). Only Christ felt it for billions of people—not only of our world but countless other worlds (D&C 76:104).

As we contemplate the incomprehensible experience of the Savior in the Garden of Gethsemane, we can notice great symbolism. In the place called the olive press, the Savior became the olive in our place. The press was the full weight of sins and infirmities of billions of people, which caused blood to ooze from the capillaries of His body just as olives give their oil. That symbolism carries over to the consecrated oil used to anoint the sick and afflicted. I have heard some state that when the oil first comes from the olive press it is red, symbolic of the saving, cleansing, and healing blood that came from the Savior in Gethsemane. During processing, the olive oil changes to the pale yellow with which we are familiar.

Oh, what mind of man can comprehend the depth and breadth of Christ's love for us and His Father? If we could but catch a glimpse of the power of that love and its resulting sacrifice, would there not be a powerful reciprocal love in our hearts for Him? The enabling power of that love is significant.

Why the Father Said No

Having just reviewed the profound suffering of our Savior, perhaps we can now consider the profound question: Why was it necessary for the Father to cause such suffering for His Only Begotten and Most Beloved Son? The Father had all knowledge and all power; why not some other way? In response to the Savior's plea in the garden, "If thou be willing, remove this cup from me: nevertheless not my will, but thine, be done" (Luke 22:42). The Father responded, "No. It has to be. There is no other way," and the cup was not removed. Jesus drank it to the last drop. Why? I have come to the conclusion that there are at least two significant reasons shown from the scriptures. The first and most commonly understood reason was to pay the price of sin so that the demands of justice could be satisfied. But what are "the demands of justice" with regard to sin? The most powerful scripture in all the standard works relating to demands of justice comes from the Savior's own words:

> For behold, I, God, have suffered these things for all, that they might not suffer if they would repent;
>
> But if they would not repent they must suffer even as I;
>
> Which suffering caused myself, even God, the greatest of all, to tremble because of pain, and to bleed at every pore, and to suffer both body and spirit—and would that I might not drink the bitter cup, and shrink—
>
> Nevertheless, glory be to the Father, and I partook and finished my preparations unto the children of men. (D&C 19:16–19)

The Savior clearly indicates to the Prophet Joseph that the eternal law of justice requires punishment in the form of suffering as payment for all sin, which results from any disobedience of the eternal laws of God. If the Lord Jesus Christ had not suffered by paying an infinite price, all of mankind would have had to pay the price for their own sins in the same manner as the Savior. The price was paid on the cross of Golgotha and in the Garden of Gethsemane for those who sinned without knowledge as well as those who sinned knowingly. Thus, those who sinned without knowledge would not have to suffer as Christ suffered, even though they broke the law. Therefore, Christ brought justice and mercy together without conflict (Alma 42:22–25). Through the Atonement, He could provide mercy without offending justice.

Is our Heavenly Father vindictive in requiring such harsh punishment of those who will not repent? Of course not! God could not be vindictive and be God. He is a kind and loving Father. Why then must we suffer for our sins? He is bound by eternal law—even the law of justice. President Joseph Fielding Smith gave insight on this question: "The Lord does not delight in punishment, however there is the demand of justice which must be met, and therefore the wicked are forced to suffer, and this suffering helps to cleanse them from their sins."[9]

Suffering for sin does not purify and cleanse as the Atonement of Christ does for the truly repentant, but it is sufficient to allow them to live with themselves in eternity, with some degree of peace in their souls.

However, the Savior's payment of the debt, the price of sin, is not totally without effort on our part. There are qualifications for all of us who are disobedient. We have to repent and be baptized before His payment will cover our sins. Repentance requires the forsaking of sin; an easier burden for those who sinned without knowledge. But there is far more to repentance that the cessation of sin. Father Lehi, in blessing his son Jacob, tells what another key element of repentance is, before one can partake of the Atonement of the Savior: "Wherefore, redemption cometh in and through the Holy Messiah; for he is full of grace and truth. Behold, he offereth himself as a sacrifice for sin, to answer the ends of the law. unto all those who have a broken heart and a contrite spirit; and unto none else can the ends of the law be answered" (2 Nephi 2:6–7).

In addition to being a key element in the repentance process that brings a remission of sin, our "broken heart and contrite spirit" are a type related to the suffering required of the Savior. Our ability to offer a broken heart relates to the second reason (in addition to His having to "pay the demands of justice") as to why it was necessary for the Father to say no. This second reason is one of the significant *enabling* powers flowing from the Atonement of Christ. It is a principle that is much more subtle and much less known than how the Savior pays the demands of justice, but it is just as important and a key element as to why the Father had to say no to His Son's request.

A Broken Heart

President David O. McKay introduces the second reason for the Father's answer of no to His Son. The *Juvenile Instructor* quotes a letter from President McKay to his son David, who lived in the East. David had asked his father to explain the need for Christ's suffering. President McKay's response follows in part:

> My Dear Son David,
>
> In one of your letters, you asked for my views on the Atonement, and I think this is an opportunity for me to attempt to give them to you. In the first place, I have been impressed with the fact that the Doctrine and Covenants says so little about the necessity of the shedding of blood for the Atonement of sin. The explanation in the Book of Mormon, too (Alma 34:14–16) is a very good one, although it leaves unanswered your query as to the necessity of it. I think the passage quoted above give the best reason, thus far revealed.

In concluding his answer to his son, President McKay stated,

> In His life and death, therefore, Christ not only fulfilled the law of sacrifice but He fulfilled every conceivable condition necessary for man to know in order to rise or progress from earthly life to eternal life. *"And I, if I be lifted up from the earth, will draw all men unto me"* (John 12:32). In this I think I glimpse, though ever so dimly, a reason for Christ's shedding His blood—in addition to the one generally offered for redemption of man from the Fall.[10]

There are additional scriptures that also support the scripture in John 12:32, which President McKay quoted: "He doeth not anything save it be for the benefit of the world; for he loveth the world, even that he layeth down His own life that He may draw all men unto

Him" (2 Nephi 26:24; see also 3 Nephi 27:14 and D&C 18:11).

Being "drawn unto Christ" by our keen awareness of His suffering is one of the great enabling powers flowing from the Atonement. But what does it mean to be "drawn unto Him"? Could it relate to His frequent invitation to "Come unto me"? Could we not have been "drawn unto him" just by the power and example of His sinless, exemplary life? May I suggest that there was no other way that would "draw men unto him" in a manner that would radically change their lives. The incomprehensible suffering He had to endure exhibited a love for us and the Father that engenders love in us to a degree that it causes a "broken heart and a contrite spirit" (2 Nephi 2:6–7).

Also, like the Nephites who remained after the great destruction of their land, Christ declares that we are to "no more offer animal sacrifices," which, by the way, was not just an ordinance of the lesser law, but one instituted from the beginning with Adam. The Savior declares what is to replace this ancient higher law of animal sacrifice instituted from the beginning of time:

> I am the light and life of the world. I am Alpha and Omega, the beginning and the end.
>
> And ye shall offer up unto me no more the shedding of blood; yea, your sacrifices and your burnt offerings shall be done away, for I will accept none of your sacrifices and your burnt offerings.
>
> And ye shall offer for a sacrifice unto me a broken heart and a contrite spirit. (3 Nephi 9:18–21)

Is it coincidental that the new sacrificial offering the Savior requires of us, which replaces the ancient law of animal sacrifice, is what actually caused His own physical death—the breaking of His heart?[11] I do not believe so! We are to place on the altar the same sacrifice that caused His death, only to an infinitely smaller degree.

What is there in the gospel of Jesus Christ that can generate a "broken heart and contrite spirit"? What are the key elements necessary to partake of the Atonement? What is meant by the requirement of "offering a broken heart"? Oh, how important it is for us to know! Remember that Father Lehi told us we cannot partake of the Savior's sacrifice without that offering. It has something to do with the manner in which we are "drawn unto Christ." It has something to do with our coming to know of His incomprehensible suffering. Two different concepts in the scriptures provide insight to what it means to have a broken heart.

First, there are over seventy-five scriptural references to a condition termed *hardheartedness,* or hearts that were hardened. A heart that is hardened, in most of the accounts, refers to a person or a people who will not listen to the Lord or His prophets. Their hearts resist the call to change and to repent. When one's heart becomes broken, that individual (or people, as was the case with the people of Zarahemla after King Benjamin's mighty sermon from the tower) opens his heart to the message born by the Spirit with a firm commitment to follow its direction.

A second but equally significant meaning relates to the concept preached by Paul: "Now I rejoice, not that ye were made sorry, but that ye sorrowed to repentance: for ye were made sorry after a godly manner. . . . For godly sorrow worketh repentance to salvation not to be repented of: but the sorrow of the world worketh death" (2 Corinthians 7:9–10).

One day a number of years ago, I was using an unabridged dictionary to look up the spelling of a particular word. As my finger ran down the column of words, all of a sudden a very familiar term jumped out: *broken heart.* I could not help but stop and see what Mr. Webster had to contribute to my understanding. One concept proposed that the term meant, "A theological term meaning to be crushed spiritually." The thought ran through my mind, "What is there in the gospel that would cause us to be crushed spiritually?" Every gospel principle that is taught brings joy and happiness—eternal marriage, the resurrection, the Plan of Salvation, and so forth. All of a sudden, the thought filled my being that perhaps as people, we come to understand the profound suffering of the Savior's Atonement by realizing that we personally contributed to that suffering. We then are "drawn to Christ." In this realization, it breaks our hearts and brings a contrition of spirit, increasing the commitment to a changed life that can come in no other way. It penetrates us to the point of not wanting to make that great offering of love, an offering made in vain. It produces godly sorrow to the point of breaking our hard hearts, opening ourselves to the commitment, and changing our lives to be completely submissive to Him who gave so much. Chapter 4 provides a parable outlining how one comes to have a broken heart.

I obtained permission from Lynn McKinley, a retired professor at BYU, to quote a sacred, personal experience that profoundly describes this process as it happened to him:

> Such laboring in the spirit I have never known before. My wife and children were away for an hour or so, visiting her mother, and I was in the house alone. I felt the old familiar earthborn loneliness but was entirely unprepared for that which came. I knelt down beside the couch, began to pray to draw the Spirit to my breast for comfort and relief. But soon I felt an overwhelming power fill my being—not a power of light and exaltation which I wanted and expected, that I'd tasted measurably before at times, but a power that seemed almost to bruise my flesh and crush my spirit with the awful knowledge of my earthly guilt. The shameful vivid memories of sins that I had committed—tore my heart apart as they passed before my eyes and settled in my bosom. I could almost feel the anguish that the Master bore for me there in Gethsemane; the aching sorrow that I felt, to know with burning knowledge every sin I had committed or—God help me—I might yet commit, had of necessity to be absolved by bitter pain within his own pure, perfect, patient body. How the sobs tore through my throat. My spirit groaned with grief. With all the strength in me I bared my soul, confessed as deeply as my consciousness could stretch and still beyond, and plead forgiveness at the feet of him, my Savior and my King. I offered him my life, whatever it was worth to him. He bought it with his blood, the blood that oozed from every pore.[12]

Could such a total commitment come without an awareness of the incomprehensible suffering of the Savior? Truly, a broken heart is the final capstone in the repentance process that provides the commitment, the purging, and the cleansing that allows a knowledge of forgiveness to come, even as Enos received it (Enos 2–5).

Some feel that they have suffered a broken heart upon the death of a spouse or a child. Some even use that term upon the ending of a romantic relationship. It is true we can feel deep sorrow through such experiences, but they do not cleanse us, change us, or motivate us as does the experience of being "drawn unto Christ" with a broken heart. Thus, another significant reason for the required suffering of our Savior is that it "draws us to Him." It is also one of the significant enabling powers that come from Christ.

The Enabling Power of Grace

The Dichotomy. The doctrine dealing with the redemptive grace of Jesus Christ has been an enigma to many for years. My view on the doctrine of grace has not only changed, but reversed itself over the last fifty-five years. On my mission, which began a little over fifty-five years ago, our standard answer to contacts who claimed they were saved by the grace of Christ was countered by quoting James 2:14–26. This passage of scirpture concludes by stating, "Faith without works is dead." Today my answer would be totally different. But I'll save that for later.

Before we discuss the enabling powers that flow from the grace of Savior's Atonement, we need to clarify some of the misunderstandings relating to the doctrine of grace. I might mention that Elder David A. Bednar, then President of BYU-Idaho, gave a devotional talk to his students and faculty on January 8, 2002. There he taught that wherever the phase "grace of Christ" appears in the scriptures, we can justifiably substitute its equivalent—"the enabling power of Christ's Atonement."

In Christian theology there are extremes on both sides. While living in Michigan many years ago, a new convert gave me a copy of her former minister's sermon, delivered before she joined the Church. Her minister presided over one of the largest churches in central Michigan. A few paragraphs from the minister's sermon illustrates the extreme on one side:

> When you live by the law, God is always predictable. This is why we like the law. We think we know what God is going to be like and what he thinks and what he wants us to do. We can corral God then

> because we've got him locked up in his own law. He has said, "This is the way it's going to be" and that's the way it has to be. But it's a lie! It's not the truth! God will be himself and he will choose to do what he will choose to do. And he would choose to love whom he would love. And we don't like it that way. You have to understand how insidiously this thing works. We are given over to self-delusions when we choose to live by the law rather than by grace.
>
> A man living by law has a measurable device against which to measure his life; the law says so. His life is like such. And he looks at the two and he says, "Ha! Ha! I'm not quite what I ought to be, so I will change myself. I will be something other than I am. I'm going to be what the law tells me to be." And so he starts living that way. And that device is a good thing. It is measurable. It is predictable. It is understandable—no surprises, no gimmicks, nothing. And so we begin to accelerate in our righteousness and our achievements at that point. And we become closer and closer to living the law and we become less and less a human being. And do you know why? Because we live by imitation and success comes to us by imitation; by being something other than what we really are. We think we are going to merit the love of God and we are going to find happiness.
>
> People, it is false to live by imitation. You can't be something you are not. God doesn't call you to the law. He doesn't call you to such phoniness. He comes to you in his grace and says, "I love you the way you are. Why can't you learn to love yourself? I accept you as you are. Why can't you accept yourself." But we don't want it that way. We cast the grace, and with it the truth, aside. We insist on being phonies—living by imitation, living to be someone else or something other that what we are. Thus, a person who lives by grace becomes himself.

The preceding statement is the ultimate statement of what we call unconditional grace. In other words, ultimate salvation comes with no effort or requirement on our part to change or live our lives to be in conformance with the teachings of the Savior. Several scriptures are used to support such a doctrine. Just two are shown here as an example. First, many use the event at the crucifixion of the Savior, when he declared to the one thief, "Verily I say unto thee, Today shalt thou be with me in paradise" (Luke 23:43). To those not of our faith it seems obvious—the thief hanging by the Savior never had a chance to repent or live the gospel, but he is going to heaven with the Savior based upon his mere acceptance of Christ. Those of other faiths do not understand that "paradise" is not the heavenly realms of the Father, but the spirit world, where the spirits of all men who die go to await resurrection and final judgment. They need to remember that three days after the crucifixion, immediately upon being resurrected, the Savior said to Mary, "Touch me not; for I am not yet ascended to my Father" (John 20:17). That was three days after He had told the thief next to him on the cross that "today" he would be with Him in paradise. Three days later Christ had not yet ascended to the Father. Where had He been? He had been to the spirit world to organize the missionary force and to take the gospel to those who had never received it in mortality (see D&C 138; 1 Peter 3:18–20, 4:6).

The second scripture commonly used to support unconditional grace is Paul's statement, "For by grace are ye saved *through faith;* and that not of yourselves: it is the gift of God: Not of works, lest any man should boast" (Ephesians 2:8–9). Many people, like the minister quoted, interpret this scripture as saying that grace is a gift of God and requires no effort on our part. A more literal interpretation of "through faith," from the Greek *dia pistose,* makes grace conditional upon being in a state of faith or in doing the things required of Christ. Had it been from the Greek *dia pistone,* faith would have been a completed effect, not subject to conditions. It is easy to see how confusing any doctrine can be by focusing on a few scriptures, without taking into account the whole gospel. The doctrine of unconditional grace is easy to teach and for people to accept because such liberal interpretations makes life a whole lot easier to live, with little effort on our part. All we have to do is verbally accept Christ.

On the other extreme, I took a book with me into the mission field (obviously a number of years ago) written by an LDS author that stated the common understanding of many Latter-day Saints at the time. The author proposed that the resurrection was provided through the grace of Christ, but salvation from sin in the highest sense came primarily through our good works and obedience. This position is what I, and most other missionaries of that day, used in the mission field to combat the doctrine of grace. There are hundreds of New Testament scriptures that can be quoted that teaches that obedience to God's law is necessary. Just a couple of scriptures will be used to illustrate. First, Jesus told the rich young ruler who desired to know the requirement for achieving eternal life, "But if thou wilt enter into life, keep the commandments." He then went on to specifically define the necessity of keeping the Ten Commandments, the need to love God and neighbors, and ultimately, to give his wealth to the poor (Matthew 19:17–21). In a second instance, the Savior described two gates: the first enters into destruction and is wide—many would enter it. The second is the gate to life eternal and is narrow—few would enter that gate. He then concludes by saying, "Not everyone that saith unto me, Lord, Lord, shall enter into the kingdom of heaven; but he that doeth the will of my Father, which is in heaven" (Matthew 7:21). If God accepted everyone through the grace provided by Christ, without regard to obedience to law, it seems to me that the gate to eternal life would have to be pretty wide, with many going in.

A third example is the Sermon on the Mount. Much of the sermon states how the followers of Christ should live their lives. In the fifth chapter of Matthew, the Savior adds a higher level of obedience and righteousness than that required by the Ten Commandments (see Matthew 5:21–22,31–35,38–41,43–44, 48). The basic message of the gospel from all the writers of the New Testament is to repent, to be baptized, and to live the gospel as taught by Christ (see John 3:1–5, Luke 24:46–47; Acts 3:19; Romans 2:6–8, Titus 3:8; James 2:14, 18; 1 John 2:3–4; Revelation 20:12). In other words, as John writes, we will be "judged according to our works." It is interesting that those proclaiming unconditional grace look primarily at Paul's teachings and totally ignore the Savior's teachings.

It is easy to see the dichotomy between the two positions of grace and works. So how is it possible to reconcile the two positions? Do they need to be reconciled? Latter-day Saints need to understand and accept the doctrine of grace. We learn from Nephi's statements: "After ye are reconciled unto God, that it is only in and through the grace of God that ye are saved" (2 Nephi 10:24), and "For we know that it is by grace that we are saved, after all we can do" (2 Nephi 25:23).

Confusion about this issue existed among members of the Church, as suggested by article that was printed in *Newsweek* a number of years ago. The religion editor wrote the article after spending time among members of the Church in Utah. He stated that members of the Church believed that the Church's position was "men were born free of sin and earn their way to godhood by proper exercised free will." He also went on to say that our belief was that Jesus' Atonement does not "atone for the sins of others."[13] When challenged by the "defenders of the faith" who wrote letters to the editor protesting the error of the author's position, the author responded he was not writing what he learned from books or Church authorities that defined the Church's doctrine. It was what he learned from visits with lay members of the Church. In other words, he was not trying to give an accurate presentation of the Church's position on various points of doctrine, but what the average, common member of the Church perceived the doctrine to be.

The thoughts that began to clear my mind of the dichotomy between grace and works, were simple questions relating to personal sin.

- What would man's position be had there been no Atonement? Does cessation of sin cleanse a person from sin?
- Had there been no Atonement, would a person's good works alone eliminate the need to suffer for sin previously committed?
- Do we earn or merit the incomprehensible price our Savior paid for our sins?
- Without the Atonement, would man's return to obedience cleanse him of previously committed sin?

We have already covered in-depth the redemptive suffering of Christ that is central to the doctrine of grace. It is important, however, to realize that without the suffering of Christ's Atonement there would have been no grace available to mankind. Sometimes it is not pleasant to contemplate the suffering He endured, particularly as we realize that the weight of our personal sins contributed to that suffering. However, it is essential for members of the Church to understand it and make it an integral part of their lives. There is no doctrine more important or sacred than that of the Atonement of Jesus Christ. It is through that infinite sacrifice that grace is provided. As we examine the elements of grace, it is easy to see that we are truly saved and enabled by grace through Christ's Atonement, "after all we can do."

Grace Defined. To intelligently discuss the doctrine of grace, we need to define what those not of our faith mean when they use the term, as well as define the Church's definition. Webster's Collegiate Dictionary defines the generally accepted Christian doctrine of grace as follows: "Unmerited divine assistance given humans for their regeneration or sanctification." The Bible Dictionary of the LDS edition of scriptures defines grace as follows: "The main idea of the word is divine means of help or strength, given through the bounteous mercy and love of Jesus Christ." These definitions are very similar, except for the word *unmerited.* Unmerited does not mean "unconditional" or "without effort on our part." To merit something we deserve it or have a right to it.

The Church defines that there are both conditional and unconditional elements of grace. But what about meriting grace? In the book of Alma, Aaron teaches King Lamoni's father the gospel, in which he reconciles both definitions of grace: "And since man had fallen he could not merit anything of himself; but the sufferings and death of Christ atone for their sins through faith and repentance, and so forth" (Alma 22:14). Aaron states that we do not merit nor deserve grace or sanctification, but that certain requirements are needed in order to partake of it. His statement reconciles the world's definition of grace with the Church's definition. Both are basically the same. The Atonement provides divine assistance to mankind to cleanse them of sin and to enable them to achieve their eternal goals. Aaron also clarifies that the Atonement, as it applies to sin, is conditional—requiring faith and repentance. In other words, some elements of grace require effort on our part; others do not.

The Elements of Grace. In chapter 1 we discussed the Fall of man in a good deal of depth, and defined the consequences of the Fall. Many of the consequences of the Fall, previously discussed define the elements wherein the grace of our Savior is required.

Physical Death. As previously mentioned, it is likely that neither Adam nor Eve fully understood what the Father meant when he said that, if they disobeyed, they would "surely die." With the restoration of the fullness of the gospel, we now know that there were two elements of death involved. One death required that Adam, Eve, and all of their posterity would die a mortal death. Their mortal bodies would return to the earth from whence it came. Of all the elements of grace provided by the Atonement, the resurrection of the body is the one most clearly understood as being unconditional. All mortals die, the body and spirit separate, and in the spirit world they are limited in actions and longingly await the reuniting of their body and spirit in the resurrection: "For the dead had looked upon the long absence of their spirits from their bodies as a bondage. These the Lord taught, and gave them power to come forth, after his resurrection from the dead, to enter into his Father's kingdom, there to be crowned with immortality and eternal life" (D&C 138:50–51; see also D&C 45:17).

It is the Father's desire for His children to become like Him. To become exalted like our Heavenly Father, body and spirit need to be reunited to an immortal state. Because death came upon us as a result of Adam's Fall, through no act of our own, that element of the Fall is overcome by the Atonement of the Savior unconditionally. "For as in Adam all die, even so in Christ shall all be made alive" (1 Corinthians 15:22). Upon resurrection, each individual will receive either a celestial body, a terrestrial body, telestial body, or a body that is not worthy of a kingdom of glory (see D&C 88:11–24). Christ broke the bands of death for all men. The Father gave the Son power to have life in Himself and give that life to others (John 5:25–29; 10:17–18). Is resurrection something that man could do on his own without help?

Absolutely not! Did it require divine assistance? Absolutely! The whole purpose of creation would have been thwarted had the bands of death not been broken (see 2 Nephi 9:8–9). The Savior did something for us that we could not do for ourselves. Resurrection is an element of unconditional grace provided by the Atonement.

Spiritual Death. In addition to physical death, men's sins would also cause a spiritual death to come upon them, wherein they would no longer be able to *dwell eternally* in the presence of either the Father or the Son. When Adam and Eve chose to disobey in the Garden of Eden, spiritual death was almost immediately imposed, and they had to leave the Garden of Eden and the presence of God and Christ. Thereafter, angels and the Holy Spirit were their teachers, who taught them the great plan of happiness (Moses 4:5–12). In addition to this spiritual death, it caused them, with all of their posterity, to become subject to the temptations of Satan. The Savior relates the following to the Prophet Joseph:

> Wherefore, it came to pass that the devil tempted Adam, and he partook of the forbidden fruit and transgressed the commandment, wherein he became subject to the will of the devil, because he yielded unto temptation.
>
> Wherefore, I, the Lord God, caused that he should be cast out from the Garden of Eden, from my presence, because of his transgression, *wherein he became spiritually dead,* which is the first death, even that same death which is the last death, which is spiritual, which shall be pronounced upon the wicked when I shall say: Depart, ye cursed. (D&C 29:40–41; emphasis added)

Not only do we become subject to Satan by submitting to temptation, and thus entering into sin, we also separate ourselves from the presence of the Father and the Son, both in mortality and in eternity. We will remain in this condition unless we are redeemed from the Fall. As Paul stated: "As it is written, there is none righteous, no, not one. For all have sinned, and come short of the glory of God" (Romans 3:10, 23). The Apostle John teaches us that "sin is transgression of the law" (1 John 3:4). Therein, all of Adam's posterity became subject to spiritual death, separated from God and Christ. Only by being cleansed through the redemption provided by Christ can Father's children return to His presence. This leads to a second element provided through the grace of the Savior's Atonement.

Becoming Clean through Christ. President Joseph F. Smith clearly defines two elements resulting from the Fall that men cannot provide for themselves:

> Men cannot forgive their own sins; [and] they cannot cleanse themselves from the consequences of their sins. Men can stop sinning and can do right in the future and so far their acts are acceptable before the Lord and worthy of consideration. But who shall repair the wrongs they have done to themselves and to others, which seems impossible for them to repair themselves? By the Atonement of Jesus Christ the sins of the repentant shall be washed away; Though they be crimson, they shall be made white as wool. This is the promise given to you.[14]

President Smith states that mortal beings cannot cleanse their souls from the stain of sin. Through the Savior's Atonement and through the process of repentance, which includes a broken heart, they can be cleansed of their sins. Read what three prophets had to say:

> Come now, and let us reason together, saith the Lord; though your sins be as scarlet, they shall be as white as snow; though they be red like crimson, they shall be as wool. (Isaiah 1:18)

> Therefore they were called after this holy order, and were sanctified, and their garments were washed white through the blood of the Lamb. (Alma 13:11)

> That by reason of transgression cometh the fall, which fall bringeth death, and inasmuch as ye were born into the world by water, and blood, and the spirit, which I have made, and so became of dust a living soul, even so ye must be born again into the kingdom of heaven, of water, and of the Spirit, and be cleansed by blood, even the blood of mine Only Begotten; that ye might be sanctified from all sin, and enjoy the words of eternal life in this world, and eternal life in the world to come, even immortal glory. (Moses 6:59)

Just as the prophets have declared that we become unclean when we sin, they also tell us that through Christ's Atonement we can be washed clean through the shedding of His blood. This divine cleansing is not merited or deserved but is freely given through Christ's sacrificial offering given us because of His love for us. All He requires of us is to be obedient to the great plan of happiness (see Mosiah 4:2–3; Alma 5:21,24; D&C 58:42). This cleansing is conditional.

Divine Forgiveness. President Smith also states that mortals cannot, of themselves, provide divine forgiveness of their sins. This gift can only come from one who is divine, the Deity who was without sin so He could pay the price of sins for all mankind. President Smith is not saying that those in the repentance process cannot, nor should not, forgive themselves. He is saying that *divine forgiveness* is essential, but must come from Christ. Book of Mormon prophets powerfully teach of the forgiveness that comes from Christ. Enos tells of hearing a voice that declared, "Enos, thy sins are forgiven thee, and thou shalt be blessed" (Enos 1:4). Another example is when the people of King Benjamin were taught about the Atonement. They were "filled with joy" for the Spirit confirmed they had "received a remission [forgiveness] of their sins" (Mosiah 4:3). Alma the Younger received a divine assurance that his sins were forgiven (Mosiah 27:24; Alma 36:19–20). It is obvious that men, in and of themselves, cannot provide divine forgiveness. Divine forgiveness is also conditional.

Suffering for Sin. A third element resulting from man's disobedience is that an eternal law of justice requires suffering as a penalty of sin. Listen to the words of Christ:

> Therefore I command you to repent—repent, lest I smite you by the rod of my mouth, and by my wrath, and by my anger, and your sufferings be sore—how sore you know not, how exquisite you know not, yea, how hard to bear you know not.
>
> For behold, I, God, have suffered these things for all, that they might not suffer if they would repent;
>
> But if they would not repent they must suffer even as I;
>
> Which suffering caused myself, even God, the greatest of all, to tremble because of pain, and to bleed at every pore, and to suffer both body and spirit—and would that I might not drink the bitter cup, and shrink—
>
> Nevertheless, glory be to the Father, and I partook and finished my preparations unto the children of men. (D&C 19:16–19)

Whenever we commit sin, the eternal law of justice requires that a penalty of suffering be imposed. Through the His suffering in Gethsemane and on the cross, Christ paid the demands of justice, an infinite price. The price He paid was incomprehensible. As previously discussed, He suffered beyond understanding, so that we would not have to suffer. Do we merit what He did for us? No, we do not deserve it! Each of us makes a contribution to the suffering He bore. Could the penalty be taken care in any other way? No! The eternal law of justice requires suffering for sin. Only Christ, through his perfect life, was the only one not in debt. Indeed we are "bought with a price" (1 Corinthians 6:20). But in order to partake of that gift the Holy Messiah gave to us, He requires something of us. The Savior told us that if we would repent, we would not have to suffer as He suffered. However, His suffering and the price He paid for us individually will have been in vain, if we do not repent of our sins. We do not have to suffer for our sins because of Christ's divine assistance, offered generously, but it is conditional.

Sanctification. Another element of grace, coming from His enabling power that we cannot do for ourselves, is the sanctification and changing of our body, heart, and the spirit provided by the Holy Ghost. Since this process can only come after we have been cleansed by Christ's blood, we then are worthy of the sanctification spoken of in Alma 13:11–12. This passage of scriptures refers to the power of the Holy Ghost that changes one from a carnal man to a man of Christ (see also Mosiah 4:1–3). The Savior declares that this particular gift of divine assistance is also conditional—requiring a broken heart and a contrite spirit (see 3 Nephi 9:18–20). Chapter 3 covers the enabling power that flows from the gift of the Holy Ghost in more detail.

Christ's Perfect Life. The final element of Christ's grace is the life he lived. Every minute of every day for thirty-three years he withstood every temptation and every buffeting the legions of Satan could throw at him. Satan knew that if he could get this one individual being to sin just once, even a tiny bit, he would have won not only the battle, but the entire war that began in heaven countless years before. His love for the Father and for us was shown by the perfect life that Christ lived. Certainly, it qualified Him as the one worthy to provide the divine assistance necessary to save us all from the consequences of sin. He was the only one not in debt to justice. Truly we are bought with a price, for He paid the price.

My Changed Perspective. Today, unlike fifty-five years ago, my answer would be a resounding yes to those not of our faith who would ask the question, "Do you believe we are saved by the grace of Jesus Christ?" It is easy to see that we are saved by grace. Without Christ's sacrifice, repentance would be futile and obedience without value. However, I would add to my answer to the questioner, that the scriptures defines two levels of grace—conditional and unconditional. A summary of the elements of divine assistance relating to the Atonement of the Savior are:

- He made it possible to reunite our body and spirit together into an eternal, glorified, physical body—unconditionally.
- He cleanses us from sin—conditionally.
- He provides divine forgiveness from sin—conditionally.
- He eliminates the need to suffer for sin—conditionally.
- His perfect life manifested His love for us and the Father—unconditionally.
- After we have been cleansed by Christ, the Holy Ghost can change our natures through a spiritual rebirth to be able to more perfectly live a Christlike life—conditionally.

In general, the primary conditions for Christ's grace to apply to us are:

- We have to gain faith in Christ and come unto Him with a deep, motivating love for Him (2 Nephi 31:19);
- We have to repent of our sins and come unto Christ with broken hearts and contrite spirits (2 Nephi 2:6–7);

- We have to be baptized both by water and the Spirit (John 3:1–5; 2 Nephi 31:12–18; 3 Nephi 9:20);
- We have to live the law of Christ's gospel and endure to the end (Alma 5:13; 2 Nephi 31:19–20)

These are the works that brings us under the mantle of Christ's grace. Every facet of salvation from grace enables us to move toward our eternal destiny.

The Joy of Forgiveness

One of the firstfruits of a broken-heart offering—the completed process of repentance—is a knowledge that a person is forgiven of his sins. Such knowledge produces an exuberant feeling of joy. When the people of Zarahemla completed their offering to the Lord, "they were filled with joy, having received a remission of their sins" (Mosiah 4:3). King Benjamin confirmed their condition when he stated: "And have received a remission of your sins, which causeth such exceeding great joy in your souls" (Mosiah 4:11).

There is no greater example in the scriptures showing the joy resulting from forgiveness than that given by Alma the Younger. He proceeds through the process of a broken heart to a forgiveness of sins. First, he relates the sorrow that came into his soul from the weight of his many sins:

> But I was racked with eternal torment, for my soul was harrowed up to the greatest degree and racked with all my sins.
>
> Yea, I did remember all my sins and iniquities, for which I was tormented with the pains of hell; yea, I saw that I had rebelled against my God, and that I had not kept his holy commandments.
>
> Oh, thought I, that I could be banished and become extinct both soul and body, that I might not be brought to stand in the presence of my God, to be judged of my deeds.
>
> And now, for three days and for three nights was I racked, even with the pains of a damned soul. (Alma 36:12–13, 15–16)

Then, as he was able to catch hold of the doctrine of redemption through Jesus Christ, his guilt was swept away and joy filled his soul:

> Now, as my mind caught hold upon this thought, I cried within my heart: O Jesus, thou Son of God, have mercy upon me who am in the gall of bitterness, and am encircled about by the everlasting chains of death.
>
> And now behold, when I thought this, I could remember my pains no more; yea, I was harrowed up by the memory of my sins no more.
>
> And oh, what joy, and what marvelous light did I behold; yea, my soul was filled with joy as exceeding as was my pain!
>
> Yea, I say unto you, my son, that there could be nothing so exquisite and so bitter as were my pains. Yea, and again I say unto you, my son, that on the other hand, there can be nothing so exquisite and sweet as was my joy. (Alma 36:18–21)

In the preceding account, Alma tells his experience to his son Helaman. Mosiah 27 relates the actual experience and the mighty change (or the spiritual rebirth) that occurred in Alma's heart.

> For, said he, I have repented of my sins, and have been redeemed of the Lord; behold I am born of the Spirit.
>
> And the Lord said unto me: Marvel not that all mankind, yea, men and women, all nations, kindreds, tongues and people, must be born again; yea, born of God, changed from their carnal and fallen state, to a state of righteousness, being redeemed of God, becoming his sons and daughters;
>
> And thus they become new creatures; and unless they do this, thy can in nowise inherit the kingdom of God. (Mosiah 27:24–26)

Forgiving Ourselves

Perhaps a word should be said with regard to the current tendency of sociologists and psychiatrists to counsel the transgressor to, "Stop sinning and then forget about it. Don't let the burden of sin weigh you down." There is no question that, without the Savior as the foundation of the "godly sorrow that worketh repentance," it is possible for the burden of sin to carry a person into a spiritual spiral downward instead of upward. It is easy to be persuaded by the power of darkness that "all is lost, why even try." Without hope, the burden of sin becomes a millstone about our neck that carries us to the bottom of the sea.

Godly sorrow centered in the Atonement of Christ, however, carries with it a powerful feeling of hope (and even knowledge) that all will be well and that purpose, joy, and peace will be restored through Christ. Read Alma 36. A person counseled to stop sinning and just forget about it, may never enter the process that brings "joy as was exceeding as was my pain!" (Alma 36:20). Why? *Because, in forgetting their sins, they loose an awareness of their desperate need that brings them to Christ.* Remember Paul's statement: "Now I rejoice, not that ye were made sorry, but that ye sorrowed to repentance: for ye were made sorry after a godly manner. . . . For godly sorrow worketh repentance to salvation not to be repented of; but the sorrow of the world worketh death" (2 Corinthians 7:9–10).

Can you imagine the psychological impact on a person who has the Spirit whisper, "I have accepted your repentance. Your sins are forgiven! You are now clean and worthy of forgiveness, so continue on this upward path."

Several scriptures confirm that forgetting your sins, *prior to the repentance process*, is not the proper course (Alma 39:7; 42:29; 2 Nephi 4:16–21). As we deeply ponder the scriptures, we begin to receive a powerful awareness of the Savior. Our knowledge of Him intensifies our love for Him, for we cannot come to know Him, through the Spirit, without loving Him. The love we feel for the Savior causes us to strive for repentance and forgiveness. As we struggle and strive, eventually we are brought to the point where our own carnality is revealed to us (Ether 12:27). We see our transgressions in relation to the suffering the Savior endured for us, and in relation to our love we have for Him. Thus, we are drawn unto Him with broken hearts in a manner that changes the center focus of our lives. The cleansing and purging that transpires makes it possible for the Holy Ghost to come into our souls to sanctify and provide the "mighty change" in our hearts—even new "fibers, new tissues, and new hearts" as President Kimball so eloquently states. Ponder President Kimball's powerful description of the experience of Enos when he wrote to the youth of the Church about what is available through the repentance process:

> To those of us who would pay pennies toward our unfathomable debt, may we remember Enos, who, like many of us, had great need.

Like many sons of good families he strayed. How heinous were his sins I do not know, but they must have been grievous. He wrote,

"And I will tell you of the wrestle which I had before God, before I received a remission of my sins."

The account is graphic, his words impressive.

"Behold, I went to hunt beasts in the forests."

But no animals did he shoot or capture. He was traveling a path he had never walked before. He was reaching, knocking, asking, pleading; *he was being born again.* He was seeking pleasant valleys across the barren wastes. He was searching his soul. He would have lived all his life in a weed patch, but now he sought a watered garden. He continues: "And the words which I had often heard my father speak concerning eternal life, and the joy of the saints, sunk deep into my heart."

Memory was both cruel and kind. The pictures his father had painted now stirred his soul. He was warmed and inspired. Then memory opened the doors to his ugly past. *His soul revolted at the reliving of the baser things but yearned now for the better.* A rebirth was in process. It was painful but rewarding.

"And my soul hungered."

The spirit of repentance was taking hold. He was remorseful for his transgressions, eager to bury the old man of sin, to resurrect the new man of faith and godliness.

"And I kneeled down before my Maker, and I cried unto him in mighty prayer and supplication for mine own soul."

He had now come to realize that no one can be saved in his sins, that no unclean thing can enter into the kingdom of God, that there must be a cleansing, that stains must be eliminated, new flesh over scars. He came to realize there must be a purging, a new heart in a new man. *He knew it was not a small thing to change hearts, and minds, and tissues.* He writes:

"And all day long did I cry unto him."

Here is no casual prayer; here no trite, worn phrases; here no momentary appeal. All the day long, with seconds turning into minutes, and minutes into hours, and hours into an "all day long." But when the sun had set, relief had still not come, for repentance is not a single act nor forgiveness an unearned gift. So precious to him was communication with, and approval of, his Redeemer that his determined soul pressed on without ceasing.

"Yea, and when the night came, I did still raise my voice high that it reached the heavens."

Could the Redeemer resist such determined imploring? How many

> of you have thus persisted? How many of you, with or without serious transgressions, have ever prayed all day and into the night? Have you ever wept and prayed for many hours? How many of you have ever prayed for five hours? For one? For 30 minutes? For ten minutes? . . .
>
> How much do you pray, my young friends? How often? How earnestly? If you should have errors in your life, have you wrestled before the Lord? Have you found your deep forest full of solitude? How much has your soul hungered? How deeply have your needs impressed your heart? When did you kneel before your Maker in total quiet? For what did you pray—your own soul? How long did you thus plead for recognition—all day long? And when the shadows fell, did you still raise your voice in mighty prayer, or did you liquidate it with some trite word and phrase?
>
> As you struggle in the spirit and cry mightily and covenant sincerely, the voice of the Lord God will come into your mind, as it did to that of Enos:
>
> "Thy sins are forgiven thee and thou shalt be blessed" (Enos 1:5).[15]

President Kimball's account of Enos's experience and how his guilt was swept away when his sins were forgiven is a landmark message on the need to seek for forgiveness. The joy in the heart of Enos was equal to that of Alma's. As we weigh the price that is asked, even that of a broken heart and a contrite spirit, we must look beyond the price to be paid to the joy of forgiveness that fills our souls and changes our hearts. The price paid is incredibly far less than the value received. In fact it could, and should, be called a gift. Can anything be more enabling than to feel the redemptive power coming from the Savior?

The First Principle

When asked to define the first principle of the gospel, many members respond with "faith." In outlining the Articles of Faith, Joseph Smith narrowly defined the first principle as "faith in the Lord Jesus Christ." Is Joseph saying that faith in Heavenly Father, faith in the Book of Mormon, or faith in latter-day prophets are not important? Of course not! In the fourth article of faith, Joseph is merely outlining the first principles and ordinances wherein men are changed from a "carnal and fallen" nature to a state where they become the sanctified sons and daughters of Christ (Mosiah 5:6–7).

It is through our faith in and love for Jesus Christ that we can repent in a manner that breaks our heart and changes our lives. Water baptism symbolizes a contract representing our commitment to take upon ourselves the responsibilities that come from the acceptance of the Savior's sacrifice. We covenant to take upon us His name, to always remember Him, to obey His commandments, and to endure to the end. Providing the Gift of Holy Ghost (the spiritual rebirth) is the ratification of the contract by the Savior. The Holy Ghost sanctifies the soul, gives us an awareness of our forgiveness and places the "newborn" son or daughter of Christ (Mosiah 5:7) on the road toward eternal life. The journey is by no means completed, for he must "endure to the end" (2 Nephi 31:20) and Satan promises to "make war" with those who have entered the path (D&C 76:29). Thus, we begin to comprehend Joseph's reasons for defining the "first principle" as he did, for it is faith in Christ that starts the process that ultimately brings about the redemption of man.

Conclusion

It was necessary for the Son of Man to suffer and die that he truly might "descend below all things" (D&C 122:8) and draw all men unto Him in a manner that breaks their hearts and enables them to change the carnality of their lives. In addition, He paid the demands of justice to keep all men from having to suffer for their own sins. The Savior inherited the ability to die from Mary, his mortal mother. He inherited "life within himself" and power over death from his immortal Father. In some inexplicable way the resurrection of Christ, the Lord, on the third day broke the bands of death for all mortal creatures. (1 Corinthians 15:22). Thus, we all will be resurrected with an eternal, immortal body. Those who live a celestial law will receive a celestial body; those who live a terrestrial law a terrestrial body; and those who live a telestial law a telestial body. The sons of perdition receive a body without glory (1 Corinthians 15:39–42; D&C 88:27–31).

The Savior thus completed all of the work necessary for the exaltation of man. His sacrificial offering made it possible that man might be cleansed of his sins and sanctified unto a newness of life—if he would repent of his sins and come unto Christ with a broken heart and a contrite spirit. His resurrection provided that man might also be reunited with a celestialized body of flesh and bone. Thus, Christ opened the way for all men, who had fallen to a carnal state, to become reconciled with their Heavenly Father and progress to become like Him in eternity. We are truly enabled by Christ and the eternal principles He restored.

Notes

1. Joseph Smith, *Teachings of the Prophet Joseph Smith*, comp. Joseph Fielding Smith (Salt Lake City: Deseret Book, 1951), 121; emphasis added.
2. James E. Talmage, *Articles of Faith* (Salt Lake City, Deseret Book, 1961), 77; emphasis added
3. Boyd K. Packer, "The Mediator," *Ensign,* May 1977.
4. Joseph Fielding Smith, *Doctrines of Salvation,* vol. 1, 130.
5. James E. Talmage, *Jesus the Christ* (Salt Lake City: Deseret Book, 1985), 568–69, 613, 620–21.
6. Melvin J. Ballard, *Sermons and Missionary Services of Melvin J. Ballard*, ed. Bryant S. Hinckley (Salt Lake City: Deseret Book, 1949), 154.
7. James E. Talmage, *Jesus the Christ,* 613.
8. Ibid., 620–21
9. Joseph Fielding Smith, *Answers to Gospel Questions* (Melchizedek Priesthood Course of Study, 1972–73), 91.
10. David O. McKay, *Instructor,* Mar. 1959, emphasis added.
11. James E. Talmage, *Jesus the Christ,* 16.
12. Lynn McKinley, *The Spirit Giveth Life* (Salt Lake City: Deseret Book, 1955), 52–53.
13. Kenneth L. Woodward, "What Mormons Believe," *Newsweek*, Sept. 1, 1980, 68.
14. Joseph F. Smith, in Conference Report, Oct. 1899, 42.
15. Spencer W. Kimball, "Prayer," *New Era,* Mar. 1978, 17–18.

3

Becoming Sons and Daughters of Christ

As the Savior spoke from the heavens to the remaining Nephites, those who were in darkness after the great destruction, He identified Himself and then told them he had fulfilled one of the significant ordinance-laws that had existed from the time Adam and Eve left the Garden of Eden down to His time. He told them that they were to no longer offer up the shedding of the blood of animal sacrifices, and in particular the blood of the firstborn lamb that was without spot or blemish. The latter were especially touching, heart-rendering sacrifices because the young lambs were without the ability to resist the shedding of their blood. These offerings truly foreshadowed and symbolized the Son of Man, who was to give Himself as a ransom for sin. He was our Lamb without "spot or blemish." But now, as the Savior spoke to the Nephites, these offerings were no longer required. To replace this sacrifice, there was to be an added emphasis and blessing on an existing requirement that the Lord had previously given to them. Listen to the voice of Christ speaking out of the darkness from the heavens:

> Behold, I am Jesus Christ the Son of God. I created the heavens and the earth, and all things that in them are. I was with the Father from the beginning. I am in the Father and the Father in me; and in me hath the Father glorified his name.
>
> And as many as have received me, to them have I given to become the sons of God; and even so will I to as many as shall believe on my

> name, for behold, by me redemption cometh, and in me is the law of Moses fulfilled.
>
> I am the light and the life of the world. I am Alpha and Omega, the beginning and the end.
>
> And ye shall offer up unto me no more the shedding of blood; yea, your sacrifices and your burnt offerings shall be done away, for I will accept none of your sacrifices and your burnt offerings.
>
> And ye shall offer up for a sacrifice unto me a broken heart and a contrite spirit. *And whoso cometh unto me with a broken heart and a contrite spirit, him will I baptize with fire and with the Holy Ghost,* even as the Lamanites, because of their faith in me at the time of their conversion, were baptized with fire and with the Holy Ghost, and they knew it not. (3 Nephi 9:15, 17–20)

What was the sacrifice that was to replace shedding the blood of lambs? Father Lehi indicated that the same—a broken heart and a contrite spirit—was necessary to fully partake of the Atonement of Jesus Christ (2 Nephi 2:7). And how was the Savior going to bless those who made that sacrifice? With a baptism of fire and the Holy Ghost. That reward must be extremely important to have been the focus of the Savior's first message to the Nephites. In the previous chapter we discussed in some depth what is required to offer up a broken heart and a contrite spirit. Now I will attempt to show the enabling power that flows from the "baptism of fire and the Holy Ghost" and also adds to the enabling power that comes from the Atonement and being cleansed of sin. Both powers are very much intertwined.

The Enabling Power of the Gift of the Holy Ghost

We often hear in church meetings that the primary blessings we receive from the Holy Ghost are guidance and direction throughout our lives, which is certainly of great value. However, the Holy Spirit has several titles. The Comforter, Testator, and Sanctifier are three mentioned by Bruce R. McConkie that add to our understanding.[1]

The Holy Spirit, as a Testator, testifies of truth to both members of the Church having the gift of the Holy Ghost, as well as those not of our faith. It is the source of testimony—the source of knowing what is truth and what is not. You do not need to be a member of the Church to receive Moroni's promise to know that the Book of Mormon is the word of God by the power of the Holy Ghost (Moroni 10:4–5). The only requirements for the Holy Spirit to bear witness of the truth of the Book of Mormon, or any other principle or doctrine, is for us to "ask with a sincere heart, with real intent, having faith in Christ." Anyone who does so is promised that "he will manifest the truth of it unto you by the power of the Holy Ghost." Thus, the Holy Spirit is truly a Testator.

Another of the titles of the Holy Ghost is that of Comforter. To eleven of His Apostles, Jesus promised a special gift from the Holy Spirit in addition to testimony:

> If ye love me, keep my commandments.
>
> And I will pray the Father, and he shall give you another Comforter, that he may abide with you for ever;
>
> Even the Spirit of truth; *whom the world cannot receive,* because it seeth him not, neither knoweth him: but ye know him; for he dwelleth with you, and shall be in you. . . .
>
> *But the Comforter,* which is the Holy Ghost, whom the Father will send in my name, he shall teach you all things, and bring all things to your remembrance, whatsoever I have said unto you.
>
> *Peace I leave with you, my peace I give unto you:* not as the world giveth, give I unto you. Let not your heart be troubled, neither let it be afraid. . . .
>
> But when the Comforter is come, whom I will send unto you from the Father, even the Spirit of truth, *which proceedeth from the Father, he* [the Holy Ghost] *shall testify of me.* (John 14:15–17, 26–27; 15:26)

Jesus explained that one blessing from the Holy Ghost to those keep His commandments (not just to the Apostles, but to all who would obey Him), would be to receive a Comforter. What are the primary conditions relating to obedience? They are having faith in Christ, repenting of sin, being baptized for the remission of sins by one having authority, and receiving the ordinance of confirmation by the laying of hands by one having authority. Had the Twelve received the confirmation ordinance?

Jesus gave this gift to his Apostles: "Then said Jesus to them again, Peace be unto you: as my Father hath sent me, even so send I you. And when he had said this, he breathed upon them [probably as he laid his hands on their heads] and saith unto them, Receive ye the Holy Ghost" (John 20:21–22).

The peace that comes from Christ through His Atonement ultimately comes through the Holy Ghost. He will teach us the peaceable things of the kingdom and bring all things to our remembrance that we have learned from Christ as we are in need of them. Thus the Holy Spirit truly provides us with peace and comfort as the Comforter.

In our church meetings, we often do not hear about the third significant blessing relating to the Holy Spirit's title as Sanctifier. Read what Alma the Younger discussed about those having the higher priesthood and the gift of the Holy Ghost:

> Therefore they were called after this holy order, and were sanctified, and their garments were washed white through the blood of the Lamb.
>
> Now they, after being *sanctified by the Holy Ghost,* [after] having their garments made white, being pure and spotless before God, could not look upon sin save it were with abhorrence; and there were many, exceedingly great many, who were made pure and entered into the rest of the Lord their God. (Alma 13:11–12)

Would we not be enabled by being cleansed of sin and sanctified so as to not be able to "look upon sin except with abhorrence"? In the scriptures the word *sanctify* has at least two different meanings. Sometimes it is synonymous with being cleansed. In the preceding scripture, Alma indicates that we are cleansed by the blood of Christ, therefore his use of the word *sanctify* likely means something in addition to being cleansed.

In giving his account of the creation of the world, Moses states that after the six days of creation, "God blessed the seventh day and sanctified it" (Genesis 2:3). It is not reasonable that God cleansed the seventh day. That doesn't make sense. It is likely that an additional usage of the word is that God "changed" the seventh day from an ordinary day to a holy day. If we assume that Alma used *sanctify* in that sense, then he is saying we are cleansed by the blood of Christ and changed from our carnal natures by the Holy Ghost. Is this not what the Savior promised to the Nephites, who would offer the sacrifice of a broken heart and contrite spirit, even that of a baptism of fire and the Holy Ghost? Alma the Younger was speaking of this when he asked his brethren of the Church: "And now behold, I ask of you, my brethren of the church, have ye spiritually been born of God? Have ye received his image in your countenances? Have ye experienced this mighty change in your hearts?" (Alma 5:14).

Thus, we have identified two powerful forces found in the scriptures that can enable all men to move forward and upward in their lives sufficiently to achieve celestial status as their eternal reward. First, it is that power that comes as we begin to comprehend the infinite suffering of the Lord Jesus Christ. This knowledge helps us to feel the depth and breadth of Christ's love for us. Thus we are "drawn unto him" with a reciprocal love that helps us to change our lives and offer a broken heart sufficient to partake of the redemptive, enabling power that is offered in the Atonement.

The second enabling power, resulting from the offering of a broken heart and contrite spirit, brings at least an initial experience of baptism of fire and the Holy Ghost that sanctifies and changes our natures. We need to understand this second source of enabling power. The scriptures and statements of the Brethren are voluminous.

The Rebirth: An Event or a Process over Time?

Before we go further, we need to address the question as to whether the rebirth experience is an event or a process. The real question is not related to the semantics of the terms *event* or *process*, but more to the questions: Is the birth of the Spirit an initial experience that I can know when it happens and record the time of the event? Or does it happen gradually as a process throughout my life and in a way that it may have already happened or be happening without me being aware of its occurring? The scriptures and prophets seem to indicate that the spiritual rebirth is neither an event nor a process alone, but a combination of events and processes. The following thoughts show what the scriptures and prophets have said with regard to these questions.

Analogy to Water Baptism. When the Savior outlined the way for Nicodemous to enter into the Kingdom of God, he declared, "Except a man be born of water and of the Spirit, he cannot enter into the kingdom of God" (John 3: 5).

In this account the Lord did not differentiate between water baptism and the baptism of Spirit. In fact in several instances the scriptures refer to this "spirit birth" as a baptism. John the Baptist, when introducing Jesus to his disciples, stated, "I indeed baptize you with water unto repentance: but he that cometh after me is mightier than I, whose shoes I am not worthy to bear: he shall baptize you with the Holy Ghost, and with fire" (Matthew 3:11; see also John 1:26–33).

Considering all of the things that John could have said in introducing the Savior and His mission, especially relating to the Atonement, it is interesting he emphasized that Jesus would provide a baptism of fire that he (John) could not provide. When Jesus first spoke to the Nephites out of the darkness after the great destruction, He stated the very same idea:

> And whoso cometh unto me with a broken heart and a contrite spirit, him will *I baptize* with fire and the Holy Ghost. (3 Nephi 9:20; emphasis added)

> And unto them I have given power that they may baptize you with water; and after that ye are baptized with water, behold, *I will baptize* you with fire and the Holy Ghost. (3 Nephi 12:1; emphasis added)

Is water baptism an event or a process? It is a profound combination of both processes and events. The actual ordinance of being immersed in the water by one having authority is obviously an event for which one can record the day and the hour. But the event has no meaning nor validity without the accompanying process of gaining faith in Christ and repenting of sins. Like water baptism, the Spirit baptism consists of a combination of events and processes that begins with an initial ordinance. Confirmation requires someone with authority laying his hands upon the recipient's head and conferring the right to receive the Holy Ghost. The "gift" itself does not come until the individual has properly prepared himself to receive it.

> Mere compliance with the formality of the ordinance of baptism does not mean that a person has been born again. No one can be born again without baptism, *but the immersion in water and the laying on of hands to confer the Holy Ghost do not of themselves guarantee that a person has been or will be born again.* The new birth takes place only for those who actually enjoy the gift or companionship of the Holy Ghost, only for those who are fully converted, who have given themselves without restraint to the Lord. Thus Alma addressed himself to his "brethren of the church," and pointedly asked them if they had "spiritually been born of God," received the Lord's image in their countenances, and *had the "mighty change" in their hearts which always attends the birth of the Spirit*" (Alma 5:14, 31; emphasis added).[2]

The ordinance means nothing without the preparatory process and events that include faith in the Lord Jesus Christ, repentance to the point of a "broken heart and a contrite spirit" and baptism by water. After the process has been implemented to a sufficient degree, other events take place—the gift of having our sins revealed to us in a powerful way (Ether 12:27) in relation to the suffering endured by the Savior; an immersion in the heavenly element of the Holy Ghost; a change (mighty or subtle) occurring in our souls; a knowledge of forgiveness; and our whole perspective of life changing. In other words, there are things that only the individual can do, some of which occur over varying time periods. Then there are things that only the Holy Ghost can do, some of which occur over time and some occur as an event.

Immersion in the heavenly element of the Spirit may seem strange and out of order until one recalls the Savior's declaration to Nicodemus and the Nephites, and John's introduction of the Savior. Remember water baptism, by definition, is a complete immersion of the individual being baptized in water. The term *baptize* comes from the Greek root *baptizo* meaning to completely immerse. In John 3:5, the Savior did not change the terminology for the Spirit birth as he explained the requirements for entrance into the Kingdom. For example, the Savior could have said, "Except a man be born of water (baptized) and receive the Spirit, he cannot enter the Kingdom of God," but He didn't. He used the same root for both water and spirit rebirths. In fact He reiterated the same point in speaking to Adam, "even so ye must be born again . . . of water, and of the Spirit, and be cleansed by blood" (Moses 6:59).

To be "born of" literally means to come out of the womb of water, in which the child was immersed before he begins his new life of mortality. The symbolism between the birth of a child and the baptism of water is quite profound. The gestation period of pregnancy prepares and strengthens the unborn child for life as a mortal being before he leaves the watery womb with the loss of some of the mother's blood. The gestation period of a convert is the time when he gains faith in Christ and enters the repentance process. This process prepares and strengthens him before he raises from the water womb (font) as a "new man in Christ," cleansed by the blood of Christ (see Moses 6:59–60).

The question can be asked, "Is a person gradually baptized in water over time?" No. It is an event that happens where the day and hour can be recorded. Now remember that the Savior makes no distinction between the Spirit Birth and the Water Birth. Might it also be possible for a person to be immersed in the Spirit in order to be spiritually reborn? Many accounts record it to be so. But remember that events and processes, like repentance, are a prerequisite before the ordinance has any meaning.

The gestation process, which includes the changes an individual makes within himself during the repentance process, occurs over time; in fact, it continues for a lifetime. Since the rebirth is sometimes referred to as the "mighty change in your heart," it may confuse some in believing that the rebirth is a single, one-time huge event never to be continued. However, the contribution of the Holy Ghost, which reveals repentance has been accepted and forgiveness awarded, and accompanied with joy, is at least an initial event, the beginning of many over a lifetime that can be subtle or mighty. The two rebirths, the actual immersion in water and an envelopment of the Spirit, are events that occur within the processes. This rebirth should not be just a single event, but one of many that occurs over a lifetime—possibly each week as we partake of the Sacrament and ponder the marvelous blessings from our Savior's atoning sacrifice.

Modern Day Experiences of the Rebirth

Several experiences of being born of the Spirit are reported in LDS literature, and they happen to everyday people like you and me. Parley P. Pratt records the experiences of his first wife, Thankful Halsey Pratt, as follows:

> My dear wife now had lived to accomplish her destiny; and when the child was dressed, and she looked upon it and embraced it, she ceased to live in the flesh. Her death happened about three hours after the birth of this child of promise. A few days previous to her death she had a vision in open day while sitting in her room. She was overwhelmed or immersed in a pillar of fire, which seemed to fill the whole room, as if it would consume it and all things therein; and the Spirit whispered to her mind, saying: "Thou art baptized with fire and the Holy Ghost." It also intimated to her that she should have the privilege of departing from this world of sorrow and pain, and going to the Paradise of rest as soon as she had fulfilled the prophecy in relation to the promised son. This vision was repeated on the next day at the same hour, vis:—twelve o'clock. She was overwhelmed with a joy and peace indescribable, and seemed changed in her whole nature from that time forth.[3]

President Lorenzo Snow relates his experience with the Spirit that occurred shortly after his baptism:

> Some two or three weeks after I was baptized, one day, while engaged in my studies, I began to reflect upon the fact that I had not obtained a knowledge of the truth of the work . . . and I began to feel uneasy. I laid aside my books, left the house, and wandered around through the fields under the oppressive influence of a gloomy, disconsolate spirit, while an indescribable cloud of darkness seemed to envelope me. I had been accustomed at the close of the day to retire for secret prayer, to a grove but this time I felt no inclination to do so. The spirit of prayer had departed and the heavens seemed like brass over my head. At length, realizing the usual time had come for secret prayer, I concluded I would not forego my evening service, and, as a matter of formality, knelt as I was in the habit of doing, and in my accustomed retired place, but not feeling as I was want to feel.

> I had no sooner opened my lips to pray, than I heard a sound, just above my head, like the rustling of silken robes and immediately the Spirit of God descended upon me, completely enveloping my whole person, filling me from the crown of my head to the soles of my feet, and oh, the joy and happiness I felt! No language can describe the almost instantaneous transition from a dense cloud of mental and spiritual darkness into a refulgence of light and knowledge as it was at that time imparted to my understanding *it was a complete baptism—a tangible immersion in the heavenly principle or element the Holy Ghost and even more real and physical in its effects upon every part of my system that the immersion by water; dispelling forever, so long as reason and memory lasts, all possibility of doubt.*[4]

Another account is related by Sister Claudia T. Goates, a member whose experience was printed in the *Ensign*.

> I was brought up in the Church, and I can't remember a time when I didn't believe the gospel was true. I have tried to live according to its teaching. But I recently learned that there is a difference between a "believing" testimony and real conversion. . . .

In the 1963 October general conference, President Marion G. Romney (then Elder Romney of the Twelve) made a statement that confirms Sister Goates's observation that conversion and testimony are not the same: "It would appear that membership in the Church and conversion are not necessarily synonymous. Being converted, as we are using the term, and having a testimony are not necessarily the same thing either. A testimony comes when the Holy Ghost gives the earnest seeker a witness of the truth. A moving testimony vitalizes faith; that is, it induces repentance and obedience to the commandments. Conversion, on the other hand, is the fruit of, or the reward for repentance and obedience."[5]

Elder Romney then goes on to say that conversion is synonymous with the Spirit rebirth. Sister Goates continues:

> When I compare my life now to the way it was six years ago, I am overwhelmed at the differences. Because six years ago—yes, even down to one year ago—I was asking the Lord night and day to take care of some very pressing problems in my life. I had begun to wonder if anyone was receiving my petitions, but I knew that if someone was listening,

> there was certainly something wrong with my communications system, because I wasn't receiving any answers. And I felt I knew which side of the system was at fault—mine.

Perhaps Sister Goates's change was not a "mighty change" like Alma the Younger, or the mighty change that he suggests in Alma 5:14. But as she writes, it was a significant change. Sister Goats continues:

> In my dilemma, with only disappointment and a humbled attitude to cling to, I finally began asking questions instead of insisting on answers given precisely to my specifications. "Why, Father, are you not answering my prayers?" I asked. And suddenly, it was as if I had found the formula. Things began to change. The next morning I felt a strong impression that my answers were in the temple . . . .
>
> Then came the rewards of our persistence. As we waited in the back of the chapel for the session to begin, I reached over and picked up a Book of Mormon. It fell open to page 141, and I read: "For the natural man is an enemy to God, and has been from the fall of Adam, and will be, forever and ever, unless he yields to the enticings of the Holy Spirit, and putteth off the natural man and becometh a saint through the Atonement of Christ the Lord, and becometh as a child, submissive, meek, humble, patient, full of love, willing to submit to all things which the Lord seeth fit to inflict upon him, even as a child doth submit to his father" (Mosiah 3:19).
>
> I read this passage many times and certainly did agree, but I thought little more about it at the time. After the first session, we immediately went back to the chapel, and again I picked up a Book of Mormon while waiting, and again it fell open to page 141. Again my eyes were drawn to the same passage. Was it coincidence? I wondered. It finally registered with me that perhaps the Lord was trying to give me a message, and after pondering the scripture through the second session, I knew the Lord wished me to be more patient and more willing to submit to those things that he saw fit to inflict upon me—including not having my prayers answered according to my desires. Still I was not satisfied that I had learned all I needed from that scripture.
>
> That night in the motel I couldn't sleep; the night seemed endless. I pondered Mosiah 3:19, but no more answers came. It was not until a year later that I realized the truth—*the scripture dealt with repentance, the subject I needed most but was least equipped to deal with in my condition.* My spirit, however, was being prepared in ways that my mind did not recognize. The section . . . was going to change my thinking, my

> attitudes, my prayers, and my life. It provided all the answers I was seeking and much more.

Generally, for most people as with Sister Goates, the path to the rebirth begins with the inspiration that we really need to become more Christlike, submissive, and repentant. This comes as we "come unto Christ" and learn of the power of His Atonement. Sister Goates continues:

> As I tried to listen to the "enticing of the Holy Spirit," as King Benjamin admonished, I felt strongly impressed to concentrate on the temple ceremony to try to understand it more fully. Suddenly, about midway through, I felt I was experiencing what the Prophet Joseph Smith describes as 'pure intelligence' flowing into my mind and heart. I began to fathom the beauty and necessity of the temple ceremony in a manner that far exceeded my natural ability. The Holy Ghost bore witness to me that Jesus Christ was indeed the Son of God. . . . I began to fathom the necessity of the Atonement in a way I had not understood before. Without the Savior's help, I literally could not rid myself of my mistakes and continue to progress. . . . The Spirit bore witness to me that I needed to repent of disobedience. I felt deeply remorseful that I had not fully understood or lived the law of obedience more faithfully. I had tried to determine, to pick and choose in my own mind, what was really important and what the Lord probably wasn't too serious about.

This initial experience generally centers on Christ and his Atonement. Then flows into our hearts how far we are from being Christlike. For most of us it is not quite as devastating as was Alma's, when he experienced three days and nights of being "racked with the pains of a damned soul" (Alma 36:15). Sister Goates continues:

> This recognition of my own weakness was devastating. I was overwhelmed by remorse and consumed by the desire to be obedient. The Spirit ripped through my protective armor and I saw myself as I really was for perhaps the first time in my life. I understood that so-called 'little sins' are just as deadly as the more spectacular sins—they would take over my soul just as surely, though perhaps not as quickly. And mingled with my shame, sorrow, and fear was an exultant, rejoicing gratitude to the Lord that he cared enough to make these things known to me before it was to late. . . .

> I then felt a great rushing warmth through my entire body and a peace, joy, and contentment unlike anything I had before experienced. Uncontrollable tears of joy rolled down my cheeks. I felt the Savior's love for me spill over into love for all others—of which I had heard others express but had never understood before. My head no longer ached. My body was no longer feverish. I had been healed both physically and spiritually.

Alma's joy was as "exceeding as was [his] pain" (Alma 36:20).

> It was as I left the temple that I realized the difference between testimony and conversion. . . .
>
> That experience was so glorious I wanted the whole world to feel this great joy. And it has literally transformed my life.[6]

Sister Goates's experience was not as miraculous as that of Alma the Younger. Perhaps her friends may not have even noticed a significant change in her behavior. It may have been more like the people of King Benjamin, who knew of their forgiveness after experiencing the changes in their hearts and desires upon hearing the king's powerful message on Christ's Atonement (Mosiah 4:1–3).

New Testament Contributions

There are many scriptural accounts of the spiritual rebirth. Sometimes we are told that these accounts are exceptions to the rule. However, are we not told that the scriptures provide the pattern upon which the Saints are to build their lives? Did not the Prophet Joseph and Elder McConkie tell us that "the Apostles and Prophets simply serve as the pattern and examples to show all men what they may receive if they are true and faithful. There is nothing an Apostle can receive that is not available to every Elder."[7]

The Apostle Peter provides a great case study on the impact of spiritual rebirth. In the four gospels, remember Peter was impetuous, uncertain, and at the time of the trial of the Savior, unwilling to risk injury, ridicule, or death in declaring his acceptance of Christ. Can we conclude that Peter had a testimony before the events preceding the Savior's death? Most certainly we can. About one year prior to the end of the Savior's ministry, in response to the Savior's questions, "Whom do men say that I, the Son of Man, am?" and then, "Whom say ye that I am?" Peter was the first to respond with, "Thou art the Christ, the Son of the Living God." Then the Lord responded, "Blessed art thou, Simon Barjona: for flesh and blood hath not revealed it unto thee, but my Father which is in heaven" (Matthew 16:13–17).

Even though the Savior declared that Peter had a testimony of the Savior's divinity that came from God, he still wasn't converted. On the eve prior to the Savior's crucifixion, Jesus said to Peter: "And when thou art converted, strengthen thy brethren" (Luke 22:31–32). Here again, could it be that the Savior is defining the difference between conversion and testimony? It certainly seems so. The scriptural use of conversion relates to the rebirth.

Compare the power of Peter in the Book of Acts (chapters 3, 4, and 5) with the Peter of the gospels, who denied the Christ to lowly servants only a few weeks before. What Peter had not received might easily justify his previous weakness. What marvelous change happened to Peter that drove out the fear, intensified the commitment, and dramatically increased his spiritual strength? When did it happen? Was it because he had seen the risen Lord? I don't think so. Even after the resurrection he said, "I go fishing" (John 21:3).

There was an event that occurred fifty days after the crucifixion that caused Peter to lose interest in fishing in the sea. Remember what the Lord told Peter during His forty-day ministry after His resurrection:

> And now behold, I send the promise of my Father upon you: but tarry ye in the city of Jerusalem, until ye are endued with power from on high. (Luke 24:49)

> And being assembled together with them, commanded them that they should not depart from Jerusalem, but wait for the promise of the Father, which, saith he, ye have heard of me.
>
> For John truly baptized with water; but ye shall be baptized with the Holy Ghost not many days hence.
>
> But ye shall receive power, after the Holy Ghost is come upon you. (Acts 1:4, 5, 8)

When were these promises fulfilled? Luke tells us:

> When the day of Pentecost was fully come, they were all with accord in one place.
>
> And suddenly there came a sound from heaven as of a rushing mighty wind, and it filled all the house where they were sitting:
>
> And there appeared unto them cloven tongues like as of fire, and it sat upon each of them.
>
> And they were all filled with the Holy Ghost. (Acts 2:1–4)

What happened just after Christ's betrayal as Peter followed Christ into the courtyard of the Jewish leaders? Even with the testimony Peter had (as declared by the Savior just a year earlier and Peter stating that same evening that he would follow Christ "even unto death"), he denied his Savior three times to lowly servants. But now, after receiving power from on high, read about Peter's power fifty days later after the day of Pentecost, as he speaks to the same Jews who had demanded the crucifixion of Christ:

> Repent ye therefore, and be converted, that your sins may be blotted out when the times of refreshing shall come from the presence of the Lord." (Acts 3:19)

> Then Peter, filled with the Holy Ghost, said unto them, Ye rulers of the people, and elders of Israel,
>
> If we this day be examined of the good deed done to the impotent man, by what means he is made whole;
>
> Be it known unto you all, and to all the people of Israel, that by the name of Jesus Christ of Nazareth, whom ye crucified, whom God raised from the dead, even by him doth this man stand here before you whole.
>
> This is the stone which was set at nought of you builders, which is become the head of the corner.
>
> Neither is there salvation in any other: for there is none other name under heaven given among men, whereby we must be saved.
>
> Now when they saw the boldness of Peter and John, and perceived that they were unlearned and ignorant men, they marveled; and they took knowledge of them, that they had been with Jesus. (Acts 4:8–13)

Right after this event happened, the Jewish rulers threatened Peter and John never to preach in the name of Christ again. Listen to Peter's response to their threats: "And they called them, and commanded them not to speak at all nor teach in the name of Jesus. But Peter and John answered and said unto them, Whether it be right in the sight of God to hearken unto you more than unto God, judge ye. For we cannot but speak the things which we have seen and heard" (Acts 4:18–20).

Peter and the other apostles continued to bear their testimony of Christ and His gospel at the peril of their lives, until most of them were martyred. He felt unworthy to die as his Savior died. Peter demanded that he be crucified upside down. There is no question this Pentecostal event fulfilled the Savior's promise of power from on high to the eleven apostles. It drove out the fear, intensified the commitment, and changed their lives. They never ceased their labors until each was martyred, except for John the Beloved, who was allowed to remain and minister on the earth to the present day.

Latter-day Scripture Contributions

The experience of Enos in the Book of Mormon was a rebirth, showing the blessing of forgiveness of sins. President Kimball powerfully presented the Enos story in a preceding section. President Kimball declared that, in addition to receiving a remission of his sins, *Enos had a mighty change, which included a change in heart, mind, and tissues.*

Alma 36 and Mosiah 27 tell of the mighty change of heart that came to Alma the Younger. In Mosiah 27, a firsthand account is given, and then in Alma 36 he recounts the event to his son Helaman. The change in Alma was from darkness to brightest day. After the event of his conversion, he describes what happened to him as follows:

> For said he, I have repented of my sins, and have been redeemed of the Lord; behold I am born of the Spirit.
>
> And the Lord said unto me: Marvel not that all mankind, yea, all men and women, all nations, kindreds, tongues and people, must be born again; yea, born of God, changed from their carnal and fallen state, to a state of righteousness, being redeemed of God, becoming his sons and daughters;
>
> And thus they become new creatures; and unless they do this, they can in nowise inherit the kingdom of God. (Mosiah 27:24–27)

Another event, while not so dramatic as Alma's unusually quick repentance process (three days and three nights of the bitterness of hell) shows how many of a population of a city or a nation were brought to a change in their hearts with one powerful sermon—delivered by a king, using the words given him by an angel. Read Mosiah 3. Interestingly, the angel's words included Mosiah 3:19 about the carnality of mankind. The angel reveals that the natural man is an enemy to God, which was the key element in Sister Goates experience and brought her to an awareness of the power of the Atonement and then to a significant change in her heart.

After the mighty messages about the carnality of man and the Atonement of Christ, the people of Zarahemla were brought to a knowledge of their "own carnal state" (Mosiah 4:2); pleaded for the "atoning blood of Christ" (4:2) to apply to them; and received a great experience in which "the Spirit of the Lord came upon them, and they were filled with joy, having received a remission of their sins" (4:3). They stated, "Yea, we believe all the words which thou hast spoken unto us; and also, we know of their surety and truth, because of the mighty change in us, or in our hearts, that we have no more disposition to do evil, but to do good continually" (Mosiah 5:2). Then King Benjamin declared unto them, "And now, because of the covenant which ye have made *ye shall be called the children of Christ, his sons and his daughters; for behold this day he hath spiritually begotten you;* for ye say that your hearts are changed through faith on his name; therefore, ye are born of him and have become his sons and his daughters" (5:7; emphasis added).

Ammon's conversion of King Lamoni and Aaron's conversion of Lamoni's Father are also powerful experiences, which included a mighty change in their natures and a rebirth. Ammon first taught Lamoni about the creation, followed by the Fall of man and the need for a plan of redemption and Atonement for sin by the Savior (Alma 18–19, 22).

The Holy Ghost initiated the conversion and a rebirth (with some help from Nephi and Lehi) of three hundred Lamanites. Their experience fit into the same pattern of the other accounts (see Helaman 5:20–49). In 3 Nephi 9:20 the Savior teaches the Nephites the basic requirement for receiving the baptism of fire and Holy Ghost (see also 2 Nephi 2:6–7).

Nephi, son of Lehi, never shared his personal experience of rebirth. However, he wrote one of the most powerful discourses in recorded scripture on how we are born of both the water and the Spirit. The information was given him by personal revelation from hearing the voices of both the Father and the Son. In 2 Nephi 31, Nephi wrote what he was told:

> 12 And also, the voice of the Son came unto me, saying: He that is baptized in my name, to him will the Father give the Holy Ghost, like unto me; wherefore, follow me, and do the things which ye have seen me do.
>
> 13 Wherefore, my beloved brethren, I know that if ye shall follow the Son, with full purpose of heart, acting no hypocrisy and no deception before God, but with real intent, repenting of your sins, witnessing unto the Father that ye are willing to take upon you the name of Christ, by baptism—yea, by following your Lord and your Savior down into the water, according to his word, behold, then shall ye receive the Holy Ghost; yea, then cometh the baptism of fire and of the Holy Ghost; and then can ye speak with the tongue of angels, and shout praises unto the Holy One of Israel.

This is a general discourse by Nephi. He is basically explaining what one needs to do to be "baptized with fire and the Holy Ghost." We need to repent and come unto Christ, take upon us His name, be baptized by one with authority, and then the promise is given. Nephi then states that, after we have been born or fire, we can speak with the tongue of angels. Does this sound like an event that happened, where we can know that it happened? If our rebirth happens gradually over a lifetime, at what point in the process can we speak with the tongue of angels? Nephi continues:

> 14 But, behold, my beloved brethren, thus came the voice of the Son unto me, saying: After ye have repented of your sins, and witnessed unto the Father that ye are willing to keep my commandments, by the baptism of water, and have received the baptism of fire and of the Holy

> Ghost, and can speak with a new tongue, yea, even with the tongue of angels, and after this should deny me, it would have been better for you that ye had not known me.

At what point in time during the lifelong process of being born again would it be better never to have been born? It certainly sounds as if Nephi is saying there is at least an initial event, after which, if we deny Christ, we are in real trouble. The rebirth confirms in our hearts the absolute certainty that Jesus is the Christ. If we deny Him, after receiving it, we are sinning against perfect knowledge. Nephi continues:

> 15 And I heard a voice from the Father, saying: Yea, the words of my Beloved are true and faithful. He that endureth to the end, the same shall be saved.
>
> 16 And now, my beloved brethren, I know by this that unless a man shall endure to the end, in following the example of the Son of the living God, he cannot be saved.

In verses 15 and 16 Nephi makes it clear that the rebirth is not having ones calling and election made sure. Calling and election assures one of eternal life. After the rebirth, one has to build upon the experience and endure to the end before he is saved. In other words, we can lose that which we have received, if we do not build upon the experience and return to our former selves. Nephi continues:

> 17 Wherefore, do the things which I have told you I have seen that your Lord and your Redeemer should do; for, for this cause have they been shown unto me, that ye might know the gate by which ye should enter. For the gate by which ye should enter is repentance and baptism by water; and then cometh a remission of your sins by fire and by the Holy Ghost.

A knowledge of forgiveness is one of the blessings that is most common among all of the many accounts of the rebirth recorded in the scriptures: Enos (Enos 1–6), the people of King Benjamin (Mosiah 4:1–3), Alma the Younger (Mosiah 27:23–29), the Savior (3 Nephi 12:2), and so forth. Nephi continues:

> 18 And then are ye in this strait and narrow path which leads to

> eternal life; yea, ye have entered in by the gate; ye have done according to the commandments of the Father and the Son; and ye have received the Holy Ghost, which witnesses of the Father and the Son, unto the fulfilling of the promise which he hath made, that if ye entered in by the way ye should receive.
>
> 19 And now, my beloved brethren, after ye have gotten into this strait and narrow path, I would ask if all is done? Behold, I say unto you, Nay; for ye have not come thus far save it were by the word of Christ with unshaken faith in him, relying wholly upon the merits of him who is mighty to save.
>
> 20 Wherefore, ye must press forward with a steadfastness in Christ, having a perfect brightness of hope, and a love of God and of all men. Wherefore, if ye shall press forward, feasting upon the word of Christ, and endure to the end, behold, thus saith the Father: Ye shall have eternal life.
>
> 21 And now, behold, my beloved brethren, this is the way; and there is none other way nor name given under heaven whereby man can be saved in the kingdom of God. And now, behold, this is the doctrine of Christ, and the only and true doctrine of the Father, and of the Son, and of the Holy Ghost, which is one God, without end. Amen. (2 Nephi 31:12–21)

Nephi's great discourse is indeed one of the most powerful, clearly stated explanations of the first principles and ordinances of the gospel of Jesus Christ. In fact, it is a lengthy discussion of the fourth article of faith. Much of Nephi's message strongly implies that the spiritual rebirth is something that happens, after which other things happens. Nephi then goes on to state that, *even after having been born of fire and the Holy Ghost,* we have to endure to the end, which includes "feasting upon the word of Christ." In other words, it is possible to lose the power flowing from the rebirth experience if we are not faithful and do not endure to the end. Is returning again to a casual commitment to obedience after receiving the rebirth the same as denying Christ? I do not think so, as long as we do not deny Christ and openly fight against the Church.

The results of the Savior's ministry among the Nephites resulted in many of them being born of fire and the Holy Ghost. After the Savior left for a time, the Twelve ministered to the people, declaring to them the teachings of Christ. The people prayed two separate times. Then "they did pray for that which they most desired; and they desired that the Holy Ghost should be given unto them" (3 Nephi 19:8–9). Then they went to the waters edge and Nephi baptized the Twelve. After which, "the Holy Ghost did fall upon them, and they were filled with the Holy Ghost and with fire" (3 Nephi 19:13).

Even the Book of Moses recounts Adam's rebirth experience:

> And it came to pass, when the Lord had spoken with Adam, our father, that Adam cried unto the Lord, and he was caught away by the Spirit of the Lord and was carried down into the water, and was laid under the water, and was brought forth out of the water.
>
> And he was baptized, and the Spirit of God descended upon him, and thus he was born of the Spirit, and became quickened in the inner man.
>
> And he heard a voice out of heaven, saying: Thou art baptized with fire and with the Holy Ghost. This is the record of the Father and the Son, from henceforth and forever. (Moses 6:64–66)

In all of these instances, the baptism of the Spirit came as an event. Some of them even show the process that requires faith in Christ and repentance. Nowhere do the scriptures say the rebirth is a gradual process. There is only one scripture in all the standard works that is sometimes interpreted to be contrary to all of the previous scriptural accounts and statements by the Brethren: "Him will I baptize with fire and with the Holy Ghost, even as the Lamanites, because of their faith in me at the time of their conversion, were baptized with fire and with the Holy Ghost, and they knew it not" (3 Nephi 9:20).

Note that this scripture does not state that the Lamanites conversion, or rebirth, was a gradual process over time. In fact the grammatical structure of the sentence seems to clearly state that they *were* (past tense) baptized with fire and the Holy Ghost, "but knew not." The use of the words *were baptized* indicates that something happened. They just did not know what had happened or could not doctrinally define their experience. However, some may interpret that although something did happen, it was so insignificant in its impact, the Lamanites were not even aware of being born of the spirit. Even if that were the case, something initially happened as an event. The phrase "baptized with fire and the Holy Ghost" suggests something very significant was felt and experienced.

In the previous LDS edition of the standard works, Orson Pratt footnotes "the Lamanites" in the above verse to Helaman 5:28–52. As I read this marvelous account of the conversion of three hundred Lamanites (verses 44–52 in particular), I concluded that these Lamanites had to know something happened to them. They just didn't have the basic understanding to define what the experience was! If this event in Helaman was the event spoken of by the Savior, this conclusion at least harmonizes the Savior's statement with the other scriptural accounts and the statements of modern day apostles and prophets. We do not know for certain that Orson Pratt's footnote correctly references the event mentioned by the Savior. However, it seems improbable to me that Mormon would exclude an incident from the Nephites' history that had been specifically mentioned by the Savior when He visited them (3 Nephi 9:20).

Statements of Modern Prophets

The Prophet Joseph Smith informs us that when someone receives the gift of the Holy Ghost, or the rebirth, a person who is pure gentile, with no blood of Israel in his veins, has his blood changed by the power of the Holy Ghost and is adopted into the House of Israel. In the same statement, Joseph explains that when the Holy Ghost comes upon a person who is of the lineage of Israel, in the rebirth process, the experience is more calm and serene. In contrast, the experience for the pure gentile is more dramatic and is accompanied by more visible signs, like speaking in tongues, prophesying, or visions. In these explanations, the Prophet implies that the birth of the Spirit is an event that we will recognize something is happening, especially if an individual is not of the blood of Israel. Read his words:

> There are two Comforters spoken of. One is the Holy Ghost, the same as given on the day of Pentecost, and that all Saints receive after faith, repentance, and baptism. This first Comforter [Holy Ghost] has no other effect than pure intelligence. It is more powerful in expanding

> the mind, enlightening the understanding, and storing the intellect with present knowledge, of a man who is of the literal seed of Abraham, than one that is a Gentile, though it may not have half as much visible effect upon the body; for as the Holy Ghost falls upon one of the literal seed of Abraham, it is calm and serene; and his whole soul and body are only exercised by the pure spirit of intelligence; while the effect of the Holy Ghost upon a entile, is to purge out the old blood and make him actually of the seed of Abraham. That man that has none of the blood of Abraham (naturally) must have a new creation by the Holy Ghost. In such a case, there may be more of a powerful effect upon the body, and visible to the eye, than upon an Israelite, while the Israelite at first might be far before the Gentile in pure intelligence."[8]

Elder Marion G. Romney, in his great discourse in the 1963 October conference defined the scriptural usage of the term "conversion" as the birth of the Spirit or receiving the gift of the Holy Ghost. He also addressed the question whether someone would know if or when he had received the conversion experience. President Romney states: "Somebody recently asked how he could know when he is converted. The answer is simple. He may be assured of it when by the power of the Holy Spirit his soul is healed. When this occurs, he will recognize it by the way he feels, for he will feel as the people of King Benjamin felt when they received a remission of their sins. The record says, that the Spirit of the Lord came upon them and they were filled with joy, having received a remission of their sins and having peace of conscience."[9]

President Romney states the way to know if someone has had the rebirth (conversion): he will feel the way the subjects of King Benjamin did when they had their experience. Were these people aware of what happened to them, or was it a gradual change that occurred over time so that they were unaware of something happening in their lives? The account is recorded as follows:

> O have mercy, and apply the atoning blood of Christ that we may receive forgiveness of our sins, and our hearts may be purified; for we believe in Jesus Christ, the Son of God, who created heaven and earth, and all things; who shall come down among the children of men.
>
> And it came to pass that after they had spoken these words the Spirit of the Lord came upon them, and they were filled with joy,

> having received a remission of their sins, and having peace of conscience, because of the exceeding faith which they had in Jesus Christ who should come, according to the words which King Benjamin had spoken to them. (Mosiah 4:2–3)

Obviously, the people of Zarahemla knew something had happened to them and reported the mighty change in their hearts and a knowledge of the remission of their sins to King Benjamin, who defined their experience for them. President Romney said those who experience conversion would have the same feelings and experiences.

President Harold B. Lee, addresses the question as to whether or not a person will know when the event of being born again happens in his life:

> The question then, that sometimes we wrestle with is: *Must there always be a visible, spiritual manifestation before one might be said to be born of the Spirit?*
>
> We have some very dramatic incidents in which this is illustrated including the Apostle Paul's theophany. . . . There are some of us that think that the same kind of experience has to be experienced by everybody, or he can't be saved. . . . Sometimes in the days of the apostles some spoke in tongues and prophesied, and sometimes they did not. The same is the case with us today. Frequently, there are no manifestations at all—that is manifestations visible to the surrounding multitude. . . . King Benjamin said, to some who had now been convicted of their sins . . . "The Spirit of the Lord came upon them, and they were filled with joy, having received a remission of their sins". . . . Then came that peace of conscience—not dramatic. No outward show. But within, the individual knew.[10]

If you carefully read President Lee's account, you will note that he clarifies that the rebirth may not always be spectacular and obvious to surrounding people with miraculous events, but there will be discernable changes and feelings the individual will feel at the time it occurs. Perhaps what President Lee is saying is that it may be similar to what Sister Goates experienced.

Elder Bruce R. McConkie writes:

> To gain salvation every accountable person must receive two baptisms. They are baptism of water and of the Spirit.

> The baptism of the Spirit is called the baptism of fire and of the Holy Ghost.
>
> By the power of the Holy Ghost—who is the sanctifier (3 Nephi 27:19–21)—dross iniquity, carnality, sensuality, and every evil thing is burned out of the repentant soul as if by fire, the cleansed person becomes literally a new creature of the Holy Ghost."[11]

Does Elder McConkie sound as if he means a little heat each day over a long period of time? Or an initial first experience, that is soul changing, even to the point of a "change" in heart?

President Benson is the only President of the Church that I am aware of to express a position that can be interpreted to mean that the rebirth need not include an event that can be experienced by individuals. President Benson provides two very powerful lead articles in the *Ensign* magazine—the first, entitled "Born of God" in the July 1989 issue and the second, entitled "A Mighty Change of Heart" in the October 1989 issue. "Born of God" very powerfully presents the need to be reborn and quotes a number of Book of Mormon scriptures and statements of Presidents of the Church. It is interesting that the second article follows only three months after the first, the very next turn for President Benson to provide the *Ensign* editorial, and that it covered basically the same topic as his previous message. Possibly to soften the impact of the first article, in a statement near the end of the second article he includes a paragraph that can be interpreted to mean that there may not need to be a specific event for a mighty change or rebirth to happen in one's life:

> The sixth and final point I wish to make about the *process of repentance* is that we must be careful, as we seek to become more and more godlike, that we do not become discouraged and lose hope. Becoming Christlike is a lifetime pursuit and very often involves growth and change that is slow, almost imperceptible. The scriptures record remarkable accounts of men whose lives changed dramatically, in an instant, as it were: Alma the Younger, Paul on the road to Damascus, Enos praying far into the night, King Lamoni. Such astonishing examples of the power to change even those steeped in sin give confidence that the Atonement can reach even those deepest in despair. But we must be cautious as we discuss these remarkable examples. Though they are

> real and powerful, they are the exception more than the rule. For every Paul, for every Enos, for every King Lamoni, there are hundreds and thousands of people who find the process of repentance much more subtle, much more imperceptible. Day by day they move closer to the Lord, little realizing they are building a godlike life. . . . They are like the Lamanites, who the Lord said "were baptized with fire and the Holy Ghost, and they knew it not" (3 Nephi 9:20).[12]

In my view the way this statement is worded still leaves some unanswered questions that might reconcile it with the statements of Joseph Smith, President Kimball, President Lee, President Romney, and some of the other sources. First of all, in the above quote, President Benson appears to imply only that the "process of repentance" for many people is "subtle and imperceptible." *The repentance process is not the rebirth experience, but the process required for it to come.* President Benson does not say that there cannot be an initial (sometimes subtle) rebirth experience that changes the carnality of man and makes him aware his repentance has been received. I do not question that an individual has to change his life generally through a gradual process of repentance, striving with increased intensity to live the commandments and coming to a powerful awareness of Christ's Atonement before the blessings of sanctification (Alma 13:12) provided by the Holy Ghost can take place. Clearly, in most instances, this repentance process takes place gradually over time, and in many instances a long time, as was the case for Thankful Halsey Pratt, who received the rebirth just before her death.

There is a condition of sanctification that relates to what President Benson is saying, wherein the Lord commands us to sanctify ourselves (D&C 43:11; 88:68; 133:6, 32). President Harold B. Lee has interpreted this to mean that we must enter into the repentance process. It is also true that the process of sanctifying ourselves can, and generally should, take place over a period of time (sometimes years) before the sanctification of the Spirit can come to us. Alma the Younger, Enos (although we do not know for sure what he had done before the experience he records), the sons of Mosiah, and several other reported experiences are obvious exceptions. Their repentance process was very rapid. Alma's took only three days and three nights of heavy-duty repentance, which came as a result of the faith of his father, Alma. (Mosiah 27:14). In my opinion, Paul is not in the same category as Alma the Younger, who was knowingly disobedient. Paul sincerely thought he was serving the Lord God of Israel, in trying to destroy the new, "heretical," Christian religion that threatened the law of Moses he knew was God's law. The people of Zarahemla is a question mark. Under the direction of King Benjamin, they may have already been in the process of sanctifying themselves for quite some time. It seems unreasonable that this was the first and only sermon on the Atonement and call to repentance that he had delivered to his people.

If President Benson is speaking only of the individual's process of repentance as being gradual, or in other words, sanctifying the individual's self, there is no disharmony between his statement in his last article and the other brethren previously quoted. There are some questions that only President Benson could answer if he were here:

- Was he referring only to the repentance process as being gradual, over time as is stated in the article? Or did he intend to also include the rebirth and forgiveness with his statement that refers to the "repentance process"?

- Is he saying that the majority of Church members will not know that their repentance has been accepted by the Lord and that their sins are forgiven? Receiving a knowledge of forgiveness is one of the significant promises in the basic messages of the Latter-day scriptural accounts of the initial experience of the rebirth experience.

- Is he saying that the Savior's promise of baptizing those who qualify with "fire and the Holy Ghost (a spiritual immersion) does not occur but is a person's own effort to repent. In other words, is the promised baptism of fire or rebirth in fact the process of changing through repentance and not a promised gift that comes as a result of repentance?

- Or is he merely agreeing that the rebirth experience can come quietly and serenely as described by Presidents Joseph

> Smith and Harold B. Lee and experienced by Sister Goates, where perhaps we, like the Lamanites, may not recognize that the peace that comes from forgiveness was really a spiritual rebirth?

We previously discussed in some depth an analysis of 3 Nephi 9:20, where the Savior states that the Lamanites were baptized with fire and the Holy Ghost and "knew it not" with the conclusion that this scripture is not saying that the rebirth is gradual.

Can the Rebirth Experience Be Lost?

Is it possible to fall back into the carnality of life after being born of the Spirit? The answer is yes! Someone, who is just beginning to ponder the scriptures relating to the rebirth, may develop a misconception that one who has received such an experience is perfect and beyond the power of Satan. While it is true that a person who has been born of the Spirit is ultimately changed from his former self, he certainly has not reached perfection and is not ready to be translated into heaven. There must be a continuing effort to build upon the foundation provided by the initial experiences with the Spirit, or one will loose that which he has received. King Benjamin counseled his people of Zarahemla, after they had experienced the rebirth, that they had to do the following things to retain a remission of their sins and their relationship with the Spirit (See Mosiah 4:11–12, 26):

- retain in your remembrance the greatness of God and his goodness and long suffering
- always remember your own nothingness and unworthiness
- humble yourselves to the depths of humility
- call on the Lord daily
- if you do this you shall always retain a remission of your sins
- impart of your substance to the poor
- feed the hungry, clothe the naked, and visit the sick

In the preceding verses, King Benjamin certainly implies that if his counsel is not followed, that which has been received would be lost. In fact the Lord declares:

> Wherefore, he maketh war with the saints of God, and encompasseth them round about.
>
> And we saw a vision of the sufferings of those with whom he made war and overcame, for thus came the voice of the Lord unto us:
>
> Thus saith the Lord concerning all those who know my power, and have been made partakers thereof, and suffered themselves through the power of the devil to be overcome, and to deny the truth and defy my power—
>
> They are they who are the sons of perdition, of whom I say it had been better for them never to have been born. (D&C 76:29–31)

Satan will make a special effort to "make war" against those who have partaken of this heavenly power. Those who do not survive the onslaught—who are overcome altogether, deny that which they have known, and fight against God and his Kingdom—sin against the Holy Ghost and thus qualify to become the sons of perdition. It is also possible, if those who do not follow King Benjamin's counsel, slip back into their old ways of a terrestrial or telestial life. Everyone has to continually strive on a daily basis to build upon the foundations laid by the Spirit or it will be lost.

The Birth of the Spirit—A Continuing Process

Those who are not close to the Savior tend to think of themselves as doing all that is required of them because they attend meetings, pay tithing, and live the Word of Wisdom. It is interesting that the closer a person comes to knowing and loving the Savior and having his life in order, the greater the realization comes to him of how far he has yet to go to achieve a Christlike life.

A number of years ago, I was reading 2 Nephi 4:16–21 early one rainy morning in Michigan, preparing for an early morning seminary lesson:

> Behold my soul delighteth in the things of the Lord; and my heart pondereth continually upon the things which I have seen and heard.

> Nevertheless, notwithstanding the great goodness of the Lord, in showing me his great and marvelous works, my heart exclaimeth: O wretched man that I am! Yea, my heart sorroweth because of my flesh; my soul grieveth because of mine iniquities.
>
> I am encompassed about, because of the temptations and the sins which do so easily beset me.
>
> And when I desire to rejoice, my heart groaneth because of my sins; nevertheless, I know in whom I have trusted.

Nephi helped me to understand a whole new measuring rod for measuring righteousness. He saw himself in relation to the Savior! He helped me to see my own unworthiness in relation to the Savior of the world.

Those who have experienced the birth of the Spirit will have become acutely aware of their continuing need for the Atonement of Christ. They realize they are nothing without it and only have value through it. They consider themselves as "less than the dust of the earth" (Mosiah 4:2) because the dust of the earth is completely submissive to God (Helaman 12:7–9). The Book of Mormon's message of the "natural man" and the "carnality of man" takes on new meaning when using the new measuring rod for righteousness and obedience (see Mosiah 3:19; 16:1–5; Alma 41:11–12; 42:10; Ether 3:2; D&C 20:20; Moses 5:13).

Thus, the initial experience of the rebirth can be a powerful, soul-stirring, heart-rendering event that will lead individuals toward perfection in eternity, if they overcome the war Satan will make with them and build upon the foundation laid by their experience with the Spirit. They must not become critical of those brothers, sisters, or Church leaders who do not seem to have had the experiences they have had. They will quietly and humbly strive to bless others with whom they come in contact.

On a regular basis, perhaps even weekly, the "new creatures of the Holy Ghost" will seek a renewal of the Spirit. At every sacrament meeting during the administration of the sacrament, they will let the broken bread and cup of water (representing the broken body and spilled blood of the Savior) take them back to the lonely garden in

Gethsemane and the hill Golgotha. Each week they will attempt to make the offering of a broken heart and a contrite spirit (3 Nephi 9:20) as they partake of the body and blood of Christ, so they may be worthy of the continuing rebirth and cleansing to sustain themselves another week. Thus, the birth of the Spirit is truly a continual process, until we are "sealed His," with our names never to be removed from the Lamb's book of life.

Sanctification

While sanctification is sometimes used in the scriptures to define the process of rebirth as has been previously discussed, the scriptures also add other dimensions to the term. There are at least three levels of sanctification mentioned in the scriptures. First, the Doctrine and Covenants frequently uses the term "sanctify yourselves" (see D&C 133:4, 62). If the Holy Ghost performs the function of sanctifying the carnal, natural man, how can we sanctify ourselves? Elder Richard G. Scott quotes President Harold B. Lee as saying that wherever the term "sanctify yourselves" is used in the scriptures, it should be read as "repent and keep the commandments."[13] This level of sanctification refers to the changes we make in our lives and the repentance process that we ourselves must provide before the Holy Ghost can finish the work. Second, is the sanctifying rebirth that comes through Holy Ghost. Third, a higher level of sanctification comes when the Holy Ghost places his ratifying seal on an individual and says, as he did to Heber C. Kimball, on April 6, 1839: "Verily I say unto my servant Heber, thou art my son, in whom I am well pleased; for thou are careful to hearken to my words, and not transgress my law, and not rebel against my servant Joseph Smith, for thou hast a respect to the words of mine anointed, even from the least to the greatest of them; therefore thy name is written in heaven, no more to be blotted out forever."[14]

The Lord adds His own statement with regard to this principle in the Doctrine and Covenants: "The more sure word of prophecy means a man's knowing that he is sealed up unto eternal life, by revelation and the spirit of prophecy, through the power of the Holy Priesthood" (D&C 131:5).

Fourth, and perhaps the highest level of sanctification, is the promise of direct fellowship with the Savior. The Prophet Joseph Smith told us that those who have their calling and election made sure will, if they prove faithful to the blessings previously given to them, be given the Second Comforter, with its direct communion with the Savior.[15] We can always strive for higher levels of spirituality and should never be satisfied with status quo.

A Summary of the Rebirth Process

By studying the accounts relating to the rebirth process, it is easy to see a clear pattern in both the scriptures and the prophets. The following list summarizes the process that are key factors in this chapter involved in the sanctification of the human soul:

- First, we come to know about Christ and are enticed by the Spirit to study and learn more until the seeds of faith are planted in our hearts. Over the course of time we become increasingly aware of the incomprehensible suffering resulting from the atoning sacrifice of the Savior. Our deepening love for Him causes us to sanctify ourselves and prepare ourselves by abandoning our willfulness and disobedience in all areas, and thus, we become increasingly submissive to God's will for us.

- That faith produces a desire to know the Savior more deeply. As we come to know Him we can sense that our love for Him increases.

- As love for the Savior grows, a desire to follow intensifies until it leads to inspiration about our own unworthiness and need for a Savior. According to the scriptures and the prophets, at some point prior to the rebirth, we must become aware of our own carnality and great need for the Savior's atoning sacrifice, and we must have a soul-rendering experience of a broken heart and contrite spirit (3 Nephi 9:20).

- Water baptism and confirmation needs to be performed by someone having authority.

- A broken heart and complete repentance comes as we see our sins resting upon the suffering redeemer—the Holy Ghost revealing to us the depth of our sins.
- With the commitment and determination that comes from a broken heart, the soul is prepared and readied for the sanctifying influence of the Holy Ghost and the baptism of fire that comes with it.
- The Spirit whispers that our sins have been forgiven, which brings a sense of joy not previously experienced.
- We see a definite change, subtle or mighty, in our perspective of life, much like the people of Zarahemla as President Marion G. Romney indicated.
- After an initial experience, we will continue to have experiences with the Spirit, as we come to Christ with broken hearts, that will provide a continuing reaffirmation of the forgiveness of sin. As we build upon the initial spiritual boost that comes from the Holy Ghost and the continuing experiences with the Spirit, we will ultimately hear the Lord say, "Son [or daughter], thou has endured well, enter into my rest." This knowledge can come by personal revelation as it did with Elder Heber C. Kimball.

Notes

1. See Bruce R. McConkie, *Mormon Doctrine,* 328.
2. Ibid., 95.
3. Parley P. Pratt, *Autobiography of Parley P. Pratt* (Salt Lake City: Deseret Book, 1972), 166.
4. Eliza R. Snow Smith, *Biography and Family Record of Lorenzo Snow* (Salt Lake City: Deseret News Company, 1884), 7–9; emphasis added.
5. Marion G. Romney, *Improvement Era,* Dec. 1963, 1066.
6. Claudia T. Goates, "Converted after Years of Membership," *Ensign,* Sept. 1977, 49–51.
7. See *Teachings of the Prophet Joseph Smith,* 149; Bruce R. McConkie, *The Promised Messiah* (Salt Lake City: Deseret Book, 1978), 595.
8. Joseph Smith, *Teachings of the Prophet Joseph Smith,* 149–50.
9. Marion G. Romney, *Improvement Era,* Dec. 1963, 1066.

10. Harold B. Lee, *Stand Ye In Holy Places,* 58–62, as quoted in the 1981 Melchizedek Priesthood Manual, 72; emphasis added.
11. E. Richard Packham, *Born of the Spirit* (Salt Lake City: Bookcraft, 1979), 12; see also *Mormon Doctrine*, 70.
12. Ezra Taft Benson, "A Mighty Change of Heart," *Ensign,* Oct. 1989, 2.
13. Notes taken from the Key Note Address, Sydney B. Sperry Symposium, BYU, 1985.
14. Orson F. Whitney, *Life of Heber C. Kimball* (Salt Lake City: Kimball Family, 1888) 253.
15. See *Teachings of the Prophet Joseph Smith,* 49–50.

4

A Parable about You and the Atonement

This is a parable about you or someone like you. It seems like you have known about Christ all your life. From the time you were a child and heard the Christmas stories, you had a place in your heart for Him. But as you grow older, you become aware that there may be a significant difference between knowing about Christ and really knowing Him. You wonder, "Do I really know the Savior, or do I just know about Him?" You come to realize that knowing about Christ is an intellectual exercise where facts about his life, teachings, and mission are learned. As you ponder these things, some insight whispers to your heart that knowing facts about the Master will likely not change your life. You can know about the Savior without knowing Him. Somehow, you also come to realize that knowing Christ will only come through the Spirit and not through intellect. Maybe repentance and forgiveness are the keys to really knowing Him. You begin to think more deeply about these things and your relationship to them.

As you matured, at times you questioned why an all-wise and an all-powerful Father required His Only Begotten and Beloved Son to suffer as He did. Through your teen years and into your young adult life, you had heard about repentance, the Atonement, and the life and mission of Christ. But they were mostly just words and vague concepts to you at the time. You were not sure exactly how these concepts applied to you. But a feeling deep inside you said there was something more, something important; you just didn't know how to grasp hold of it. Over the years you made attempts to increase its meaning in your life—but a lingering feeling told you more was to be gained. Occasionally you asked yourself, "Have I really brought the power of the Atonement into my life?" But you didn't quite know the answer. You knew about Gethsemane, Golgotha, and the empty tomb; but how do they become a part of you? One day you opened your scriptures to D&C 64:10: "I, the Lord, will forgive whom I will forgive, but of you it is required to forgive all men."

For the first time, the first phrase of that scripture catches your attention and you ask yourself, "Has the Savior forgiven me?" Sometime later you open up a book by Robert Millet, *By Grace Are Ye Saved,* You open it to the introduction and read:

> Some years ago I sat with my counselors in a bishopric meeting. The session was drawing to a close because sacrament meeting would be starting in just ten minutes. A knock came at the door as we were making our way out of the office into the foyer. A young woman from my ward was there, who asked if she could visit with me for a moment. I indicated that we could chat for a bit, but that sacrament meeting would be starting soon. She assured me that we would be together for only a minute or two.
>
> After we had been seated for a few seconds, she said: "Bishop, I need to confess a sin."
>
> I was startled with the suddenness of the statement, but, managing to hold my composure, I offered the following: "Well, that could take some time, couldn't it? Shall we meet after the block meetings today?"
>
> She quickly responded: "Oh no! This will only take a second."
>
> I nodded and asked her to go ahead, and she proceeded to describe in some detail a very serious moral transgression in which she had been involved. It was now about one minute before the meetings were to start, and so I tried again: "Why don't we get together after priesthood and Relief Society meetings."
>
> She then staggered me with, "Well, I don't know why we would need to, unless it would be helpful to you, or something."
>
> I indicated that such a meeting might prove beneficial to both of us. She agreed to return.
>
> Three hours later, and after we had exchanged a few pleasantries, I asked her, "How do you feel about what has happened?"

> She responded, "Just fine." I must have shown my perplexity, because she added: "For a number of hours I felt bad about what had happened, but it's okay now because I've repented."
>
> I couldn't ask the question fast enough, "What do you mean when you say that you have repented?" (She had explained to me earlier that the transgression had taken place on Friday night, and it was now Sunday afternoon.)
>
> At that point, she reached into her purse, rearranged a few items, and retrieved a yellow sheet of legal-size paper. Pointing one by one to various headings that began with R, she said, "I've done this, and this and this, and this, and finally I've confessed to you. I've repented."
>
> "It seems to me that you have skipped an R; that your list is missing something," I said.
>
> "A startled but persistent look was in her eyes, and I noted a slight impatience with me as she said, "No, that can't be. I have everything listed here!"
>
> "The R you're missing," I responded, "is Redeemer."[1]

You agree with Bishop Millet that something seamed to be missing, but what was it? What had the young lady forgotten in her plan for repentance? What did Bishop Millet mean when he said, "Redeemer"?

More time passes. Then while at a Church fireside, you listen to a speaker quote Elder Vaughn J. Featherstone:

> I invited the young man into my office, after his having been cleared by his bishop and stake president (as a missionary candidate), I said to him: "Apparently there has been a major transgression in your life. That's why I am involved in this interview. Would you mind being very frank and open with me and tell me what that transgression was?"
>
> With head held high and in a haughty manner, he responded, "There isn't anything I haven't done."
>
> I responded, 'Well, then, let's be more specific. Have you been involved in fornication?"
>
> Very sarcastically, he said, "I told you I've done everything."
>
> I asked, "Was it a single experience, or did it happen with more than one girl and more than once?"
>
> And again he said, sarcastically, "Many girls and so many times I could not number them."
>
> I said, "I would to God your transgression was not so serious."

"Well it is," he replied.

"How about drugs?"

"I told you I've done everything."

Then I said, 'What makes you think you're going on a mission?"

"Because I have repented," he replied. "I haven't done any of these things for a year. I know I'm going on a mission because my patriarchal blessing says I'm going on a mission. I've been ordained an elder, I've lived the way I should this past year, and I know that I'm going on a mission."

I looked at the young man sitting across the desk: twenty-one years old, laughing, sarcastic, haughty, with an attitude far removed from sincere repentance. And I said to him: "My dear young friend, I'm sorry to tell you this, but you are not going on a mission. Do you suppose we could send you out with your braggadocio attitude about this past life of yours, boasting of your escapades? Do you think we could send you out with the fine, clean young men who have never violated the moral code, who have kept their lives clean and pure and worthy so that they could go on missions?"

I repeated: "You're not going on a mission. In fact," I said, "you shouldn't have been ordained an elder and you really should have been tried for your membership in the Church.

"What you have committed is a series of monumental transgressions," I continued. "You haven't repented; you've just stopped doing something. Someday, after you have been to Gethsemane and back, you'll understand what true repentance is."

At this the young man started to cry. He cried for about five minutes, and during that time I didn't say a word. I just sat and waited as this young man cried.

Finally he looked up and said, "I guess I haven't cried like that since I was five years old."

I told him: "If you had cried like that the first time you were tempted to violate the moral code, you may well have been going on a mission today. Now, I'm sorry; I hate to be the one to keep you from realizing your goal. I know it will be hard to go back to your friends and tell them you are not going on a mission."

"After you have been to Gethsemane," I continued, "you'll understand what I mean when I say that every person who commits a major transgression must also go to Gethsemane and back before he is forgiven."

The young man left the office, and I'm sure he wasn't very pleased.

I had stood in his way and kept him from going on a mission.

About six months later, I was down in Arizona speaking at the institute at Tempe. After my talk many of the institute members came down the aisles to shake hands. As I looked up I saw this young man—the non-repentant transgressor—coming down the aisle toward me, and at that moment the details of my interview with him came back through my mind. I recalled his braggadocio attitude, his sarcasm, his haughtiness.

I reached down to shake hands with him, and as he looked up I could see that something wonderful had taken place in his life. Tears streamed down his cheeks. An almost holy glow came from his countenance. I said to him, "You've been there, haven't you?"

And through the tears he said, "Yes, Bishop Featherstone, I've been to Gethsemane and back."

"I know," I said. "It shows in your face. I believe now that the Lord has forgiven you."

He responded, "I'm more grateful to you than you'll ever know for not letting me go on a mission. It would have been a great disservice to me. Thanks for helping me."[2]

After hearing this message, you feel you are getting closer to the answer you desire. You ponder Elder Featherstone's questions: "Have I been to my Gethsemane? Have I really repented?"

More time passes, but the desires within you do not subside. Then one day you pick up an old issue of the *New Era* and notice President Spencer W. Kimball's article to the youth of the Church about prayer. As you read, more understanding begins to shine through as he relates the story of Enos in the Book of Mormon:

To those of us who would pay pennies toward our unfathomable debt, may we remember Enos, who, like many of us, had great need. Like many sons of good families, he strayed. How heinous were his sins I do not know, but they must have been grievous. He wrote, "And I will tell you of the wrestle which I had before God, before I received a remission of my sins." The account is graphic, his words impressive.

"Behold, I went to hunt beasts in the forests."

But no animals did he shoot or capture. He was traveling a path he had never walked before. He was reaching, knocking, asking, pleading; he was being born again.

He was seeking the pleasant valleys across the barren wastes. He was searching his soul. He would have lived all his life in a weed patch, but now he sought a watered garden. He continues:

"And the words which I had often heard my father speak concerning eternal life, and the joy of the saints, sunk deep into my heart."

Memory was both cruel and kind. The pictures his father had painted now stirred his soul. He was warmed and inspired. Then memory opened the doors to his ugly past. His soul revolted at the reliving of the baser things, but yearned now for the better. A rebirth was in process. It was painful but rewarding:

"And my soul hungered."

The spirit of repentance was taking hold. He was remorseful for his transgressions, eager to bury the old man of sin, to resurrect the new man of faith, of godliness.

"And I kneeled down before my Maker, and I cried unto him in mighty prayer and supplications for mine own soul."

He had now come to realize that no one can be saved in his sins, that no unclean thing can enter into the kingdom of God, that there must be a cleansing, that stains must be eliminated, new flesh over scars. He came to realize there must be a purging, a new heart in a new man. He knew it was not a small thing to change hearts, and minds and tissues. He writes:

"And all day long did I cry unto him."

Here is no casual prayer; here no trite, worn phrases; here no momentary appeal. All the day long, with seconds turning into minutes, and minutes into hours, and hours into an "all day long." But when the sun had set, relief had still not come, for repentance is not a single act, nor forgiveness an unearned gift. So precious to him was communication with, and approval of, his Redeemer that his determined soul pressed on without ceasing.

"Yea, and when the night came, I did still raise my voice high that it reached the heavens."

Could the Redeemer resist such determined imploring? How many of you have thus persisted? How many of you, with or without serious transgressions, have ever prayed all day and into the night? Have you ever wept and prayed for many hours? How many of you have ever prayed for five hours? For one? For thirty minutes? For ten minutes?

My missionary prospect with his errors had prayed occasionally for seconds. Yet with a heavy debt to pay he had expected forgiveness of his sins. He offered pennies to pay the debt of thousands of dollars. He

> wanted much for little. He desired to cancel his debt without payment of principal or interest.
>
> How much do you pray, my young friends? How often? How earnestly? If you should have errors in your life, have you wrestled before the Lord? Have you found your deep forest full of solitude? How much has your soul hungered? How deeply have your needs impressed your heart? When did you kneel before your Maker in total quiet? For what did you pray—your own soul? How long did you thus plead for recognition—all day long? And when the shadows fell, did you still raise your voice in mighty prayer, or did you liquidate it with some trite word and phrase?
>
> As you struggle in the spirit and cry mightily and covenant sincerely, the voice of the Lord God will come into your mind, as it did to that of Enos:
>
> "Thy sins are forgiven thee and thou shalt be blessed" (Enos 1:5).[3]

You think aloud to yourself and say, "Wow, I really can be forgiven of my sins and know for sure." The spirit is beginning to take hold on your heart. You begin to search Atonement references in the Book of Mormon. One of the very first you look at is 2 Nephi 2:6–7: "Wherefore, redemption cometh in and through the Holy Messiah; for he is full of grace and truth. Behold, he offereth himself a sacrifice for sin, to answer the ends of the law, unto all those who have a broken heart and a contrite spirit; and unto none else can the ends of the law be answered."

For the first time you notice that only those who come with "a broken heart and a contrite spirit" can partake of the Savior's sacrifice. You ask, "But what is a broken heart? I thought the gospel was supposed to make you happy!" You determine to find out what is meant by a broken heart. You begin to study and pray more intensely. You continue to read the scriptures and the statements of the prophets with regard to the Atonement. You had never thought much about the intense suffering of the Savior until you read some statements by the Brethren:

> A great many people have an idea that when he was on the cross, and nails were driven into his hands and feet, that was his great suffering. His great suffering was before he ever was placed upon the cross. It

was in the Garden of Gethsemane that the blood oozed from the pores of his body: "Which suffering caused myself, even God, the greatest of all, to tremble because of pain, and to bleed at every pore, and to suffer both body and spirit—and would that I might not drink the bitter cup, and shrink."

That was not when he was on the cross; that was in the garden. That is where he bled from every pore in his body.

Now I cannot comprehend that pain. I have suffered pain, you have suffered pain and sometimes it has been quite severe; but I cannot comprehend pain, which is mental anguish more than physical, that would cause blood, like sweat, to come out upon the body. It was something terrible, something terrific; so we can understand why he would cry unto his Father, "If it be possible, let this cup pass from me: nevertheless not as I will, but as thou wilt."[4]

Then in *Jesus the Christ* you read a statement by Elder James E. Talmage:

Christ's agony in the garden is unfathomable by the finite mind, both as to intensity and cause. The thought that He suffered through fear of death is untenable. Death to Him was preliminary to resurrection and triumphal return to the Father from whom He had come, and to a state of glory even beyond what He had before possessed; and, moreover, it was within His power to lay down His life voluntarily. He struggled and groaned under a burden such as no other being who has lived on earth might even conceive as possible. It was not physical pain, nor mental anguish alone, that caused Him to suffer such torture as to produce an extrusion of blood from every pore; but a spiritual agony of soul such as only God was capable of experiencing. No other man, however great his powers of physical or mental endurance, could have suffered so; for his human organism would have succumbed, and syncope would have produced unconsciousness and welcome oblivion. In that hour of anguish Christ met and overcame all the horrors that Satan, "the prince of this world" could inflict. The frightful struggle incident to the temptations immediately following the Lord's baptism was surpassed and overshadowed by this supreme contest with the powers of evil.

At the ninth hour, or about three in the afternoon, a loud voice, surpassing the most anguished cry of physical suffering issued from the central cross, rending the dreadful darkness. It was the voice of the Christ: "Eloi, Eloi, lama sabachthani? which being interpreted, My

> God, my God, why hast thou forsaken me?" What mind of man can fathom the significance of that awful cry? It seems, that in addition to the fearful suffering incident to crucifixion, the agony of Gethsemane had recurred, intensified beyond human power to endure. In that bitterest hour the dying Christ was alone, alone in the most terrible reality. That the supreme sacrifice of the Son might be consummated in all its fullness, the Father seems to have withdrawn the support of His immediate presence, leaving the Savior of men the glory of complete victory over the forces of sin and death.
>
> If the soldier's spear was thrust into the left side of the Lord's body and actually penetrated the heart, the outrush of "blood and water" observed by John is further evidence of a cardiac rupture; for it is known that in the rare instances of death resulting from the breaking of any part of the wall of the heart, blood accumulates within the pericardium, and there undergoes a change by which the corpuscles separate as a partially clotted mass from the almost colorless, watery serum. . . .
>
> The present writer believes that the Lord Jesus died of a broken heart. The Psalmist sang in dolorous measure according to his inspired prevision of the Lord's passion: "Reproach hath broken my heart; and I am full of heaviness: and I looked for some to take pity, but there was none; and for comforters, but I found none."[5]

Finally, you discover the Savior's own statement about his suffering:

> For behold, I, God, have suffered these things for all, that they might not suffer if they would repent;
>
> But if they would not repent they must suffer even as I;
>
> Which suffering caused myself, even God, the greatest of all, to tremble because of pain, and to bleed at every pore, and to suffer both body and spirit—and would that I might not drink the bitter cup, and shrink—
>
> Nevertheless, glory be to the Father, and I partook and finished my preparations unto the children of men. (D&C 19:16–19)

You are deeply impressed for the first time how infinite and incomprehensible His suffering was. You are beginning to see that you were part of the incomprehensible burden he endured. But you are still not quite sure how it all fits together and still wonder why the Father would require such suffering of His Only Begotten Son.

You decide to make a concerted effort to obtain forgiveness. Your commitment and willingness to live the gospel more completely "becomes your quest." Your prayers and fasting are more determined. One evening your prayers are a little longer and a little more intense than usual, for you really desire to know and feel the power of the Atonement. After a time you become very tired and crawl into bed and quickly go to sleep. In the dreams of the night you see yourself praying by your bedside. Suddenly your room begins to grow light; your bosom almost bursts with love as you recognize that in the light is standing your Lord and Savior. You fall at his feet with feelings of worship and gratitude.

Then you see Him gesture for you to arise and you are embraced by His love. He says, "I have heard your prayers asking for forgiveness." Your heart leaps. You think, *Maybe I have paid a sufficient price; maybe I'm ready.* You answer, "Oh yes! Can you forgive me?" He answers, "There is just one more thing you have to do." You answer, "Anything you ask! Anything!" His answer startles you: "You must take me by the hand and together we will walk back through the corridors of your life." "Oh my! Is that necessary?" You wonder whether you can endure walking with the Savior along some of the paths you have taken in your life and even see some of the thoughts you have had. But, with his gentle encouragement, you pull your courage together, throw back your shoulders, and proceed.

You take his hand and begin the journey. Everything goes well for quite a while, for you have really been trying very hard to qualify for His blessings. But then you realize coming up around the next corner is an incident in your life of which you are not proud. You slow down, but again, with gentle encouragement, you proceed.

There it is! Shame and embarrassment fill your being. You can't look at the Savior as you hide your face from Him. But out of the corner of your eye, you see that He is no longer standing by your side and that He is no longer smiling. You see that being whom you have grown to love more deeply than you even realized, kneeling on the ground; agony and sorrow are written on His face; and blood is coming from the pores of his body. You see your Lord and Savior suffering for your disobedience. Embarrassment and shame melt away, and your own heart begins to break for the pain and suffering you are causing Him, whom you love. He is suffering as you have never seen anyone suffer before, and because of what you have done.

The same thing happens, as one by one you review the events of your life of which you are ashamed. Finally your heart breaks. You offer your life and your agency to Him, without reservation, because you recognize that he has purchased you with His blood. Then you feel the cleansing power of the Savior. You feel clean! Your joy overwhelms your pain and you know that you can never be the kind of person that you were before.

You awake! Your pillow is wet with your tears. But you still feel the power and understanding that came to you in the dreams of the night. Now it all fits together. You know what a broken heart is because you have felt it. You know the great joy of having your sins remitted. You feel like a new person. Perhaps you are, for you have put off the natural man and have become a saint through the Atonement of Christ (Mosiah 3:19). You feel like running and shouting to the world what you have come to know and feel. But, reason prevails, for you know that the world wouldn't understand. For the first time, you feel that in a very powerful way you know the Savior. It was a difficult journey, but, oh, the result and the value of the effort is beyond question.

Now you understand why it was necessary for the Savior to suffer as He did. You know, without that sacrifice, your heart would not have been broken and your life changed. You see clearly now there were two primary reasons that made His suffering necessary. First, the eternal law of justice, which requires suffering for sin, had to be paid by the Savior, or you would have had to pay the price: "For behold, I, God, have suffered these things for all, that they might not suffer if they would repent; but if they would not repent they must suffer even as I" (D&C 19:16–17).

It is now clear from your experience what the second reason for

His suffering was: you have been drawn to Him in a way that could come in no other way. Some scriptures come back to your mind:

> And my Father sent me that I might be lifted up upon the cross; and after that I had been lifted up upon the cross, that I might draw all men unto me. (3 Nephi 27:14)

> And I, if I be lifted up from the earth, will draw all men unto me. (John 12:32)

You also have come to realize that carrying the weight of sin without a hope in Christ carries one down to the depths of despair, while having an awareness of your sins, with a knowledge of the power of the Atonement, moves you toward Christ with a confidence and peace of mind that all will be well. You personally have come to know and feel the infinite love that the Savior has shown for all of Father's children by the suffering He endured, for you were "drawn to Him" in a manner that changed you. In a very real sense you have come to know Him and know of the depth of His love for you personally. *You have felt His redemptive power and you have been enabled.* You also know from the scriptures that the future will not be easy, because Satan will make war with those who have experienced the redemptive power of the Atonement (D&C 76). You will have to endure to the end.

To have forgiveness of sins, it is not necessary for a person to behold the Savior, even in dreams. But it is clear, as Elder Maxwell states, that it is possible:

> In the agonizing atoning process, Jesus let His will be "swallowed up in the will of the Father" (Mosiah 15:7). [The] redeeming Jesus also "poured out his soul unto death" (Mosiah 14:12; Isaiah 53:12; D&C 38:4). Another fundamental scripture describes Jesus' having trodden the winepress of the "fierceness of the wrath of the Almighty God." (Revelation 19:15; D&C 88:106, 76:107, 133:50). Given the "fierceness" Christ endured for us, we cannot expect a discipleship of unruffled easiness. As we seek forgiveness, for example, repentance can be a rough-hewn regimen to bear.
>
> The infinite Atonement is so vast and universal, but finally, it is so very personal! Mercifully, through the Atonement we can be forgiven

and, very importantly, *we can know that we have been forgiven*—that final, joyous emancipation from error.

By utilizing the Atonement, we access the gifts of the Holy Ghost, which "filleth with hope and perfect love" (Moroni 8:26). None of us can afford to be without that needed hope and love in the treks through our Sinais of circumstance![6]

Notes

1. Robert Millet, *By Grace Are Ye Saved* (Salt Lake City: Deseret Book, 1989), 1–2.
2. Vaughn J. Featherstone, *A Generation of Excellence: A Guide for Parents and Youth Leaders* (Salt Lake City: Bookcraft, 1975), 156–59.
3. Spencer W. Kimball, "Prayer," *New Era,* Mar. 1978, 17–18.
4. Joseph Fielding Smith; *Doctrines of Salvation,* vol. 1, 130.
5. James E. Talmage, *Jesus the Christ,* 568–69,613, 620–21.
6. Neal A. Maxwell, "Plow in Hope," *Ensign,* May 2001, 60–61; emphasis added.

5

Obedience Enabled by Love

A number of years ago my wife and I were among a few couples who chaperoned a group of young women from our ward on a trip from Michigan to the New York City Worlds Fair and Washington, DC. On the long trip back home, a very bright young lady, who was in my early morning seminary class, raised a question that caused me to think more deeply about an important point of doctrine.

We were driving along when Susan asked me, "Brother Packham, why should we obey the principles taught to us by the Church?" Having no idea where Susan was heading with her question, I gave her the quick, easy answer off the top of my head, "So we can achieve the celestial kingdom with our Heavenly Father." I know that she said to herself, "Ah-ha, gotcha!" But she tactfully phrased her next question to her seminary teacher: "But, Brother Packham, do you mean to say that the whole basis for obedience is founded on selfish motivation?" At that moment, I knew the feeling a pilot has when hit with enemy fire. I was "shot down in flames"! I was able to recover, somewhat, after some fast, concentrated, and deeper thought on Susan's question. I said, "Susan, you raise an excellent point. The end result of obeying the principles of the gospel is the reward of celestial glory, but that really isn't the most significant basis for personal obedience."

Susan's question is one that is quite profound. What is the most secure basis for personal obedience? Should it be based upon a selfish desire for an eternal reward? As I thought more deeply about the question over the years, I have become even more convinced of the significance of her question. What I explained to Susan was the foundation for the following thoughts that show the enabling power flowing from the love of the Savior. What basis provides the strongest motivation to be more completely submissive to the desires of our Heavenly Father and our Savior?

Why Obedience?

There are at least five criteria upon which we might base spiritual obedience:

- After Susan's second, more profound question, the thought came to me that the Savior Himself gave the most important criteria for obedience: "If ye love me, keep my commandments" (John 14:15).
- Others may be motivated by the promise of an eternal reward.
- Frequently we hear the comment, "What harm will it do?" when someone is deciding whether to be obedient or not. In other words, if we don't see any harmful results, it must be okay, or at least not that bad.
- Some may be motivated by the fear of punishment.
- Others may feel bound or obligated to obey by a sense of duty or loyalty to parents, spouses, or close friends.

If Ye Love Me. We have previously discussed in great depth that the love of the Savior is one of the great enabling powers that flow from His Atonement and the rebirth. Why might the Savior's criteria, "If ye love me, keep my commandments," be the only sure foundation as the basis for obedience? Is He not saying that obedience flows from love? Love and testimony are very closely intertwined, for both come from the Holy Ghost to the point that it would be difficult to separate them. In fact is not charity, the pure love of Christ, one of the most significant gifts of the Spirit? When we have in our hearts a deep-seated love of

Christ, we then begin to obey based upon our love. Perhaps it is at that time, we would fall within the group about whom President Ezra Taft Benson spoke: "When obedience ceases to be an irritant and becomes our quest, in that moment God will endow us with power."[1] When our love for the Savior reaches a sufficient level that comes from a "broken heart and a contrite spirit," a "spiritual rebirth" causes obedience to become a quest, and no longer an irritant. Obedience, love of Christ, a broken heart, and a spiritual rebirth are all intertwined together.

Another reason that a love of Christ is the most secure foundation is that, even if we do not see the harm in something or do not understand the reason for the instruction, we obey because we love Christ more than we love ourselves. Love is the only emotion that outweighs our own selfish, carnal desires and interests. It is the only thing that will cause us to endure persecution, sacrifice, pain, suffering, or discomfort that might occasionally come from obedience. Here are some examples that show the power of love to produce obedience, even when the consequences might be unpleasant and even painful or fatal.

Do you think the Savior really wanted to endure the suffering in Gethsemane and on the cross at Golgotha? What did He say as the suffering began in Gethsemane? "Abba Father, all things are possible unto thee; take away this cup from me: nevertheless not what I will, but what thou wilt" (Mark 14:36). It must have been necessary, for the Father required Him to drink it to the last drop. Why did Jesus obey and proceed with His suffering during those hours in Gethsemane and then on the cross? It was only the power of His love for us and for the Father that caused Him to do what He did.

Do you think the Twelve Apostles in the days of Christ, and also some of our leaders in our day, wanted to be persecuted, beaten, ridiculed, or martyred? Why did they do it? For an eternal reward? They did it because they had come to know and love Christ with all their hearts. They did it for Him. It is recorded that Peter refused to be crucified in the same manner as the Savior, because he felt unworthy to die as the Savior died. He insisted on being crucified upside down. Was that not a true act of love?

Do you think the early Saints of our day enjoyed being driven from New York to Kirtland, from Kirtland to Jackson County, from Jackson County to Far West, from Far West to Nauvoo, and from Nauvoo to the desert wasteland of the Great Salt Lake Basin? Each time they were giving up homes, families, gardens, and businesses at great sacrifice and suffering. Do you think it was the thought of an eternal reward that kept them going? Again, I think not. I believe for the most part, it was the love they had for the Lord and the prophet that flowed from their testimonies.

A friend and I saw the movie, *Saving Private Ryan,* that was based upon a true event. It had a powerful message that every young person under the age of fifty ought to see and understand. Private Ryan was in the middle of the battle of Europe during World War II. Three of his brothers had already been killed in other battles of the war, leaving him as the only remaining child of a widowed mother. The General of the Army, George Marshall, ordered that Private Ryan be removed from combat and the danger of battle. A squad of men were asked to volunteer to carry out their Commanding General's order. Every man in the squad was well aware that their assignment could likely result in death. Why did they go, knowing that they would not likely return? Because of love of country, home, and honor. I believe not one of them was thinking of their eternal reward. Perhaps they thought more of Private Ryan and his mother, who had already lost three sons, than they did of their own well-being.

Parents who risk their lives to save a child, a spouse, or sometimes even a stranger in danger are a profound example of how love causes people to give totally of themselves for the benefit of someone other than themselves.

Let me stress again that the power of love can motivate one to do things that nothing else would, especially when actions would place our life at risk and even where there is no immediate reward forthcoming.

To Gain an Eternal Reward. Next, let's discuss gaining an eternal reward as a basis for obedience. Why is seeking an eternal reward a more shaky foundation for obedience than love for the Savior? In my view, the motivation of an eternal reward in heaven frequently becomes lost in the distant view. In addition to the morality issue of a "selfish desire" that Susan asked about, an additional factor occurs: a desire for a distant reward may diminish when a selfish desire providing a more immediate and pleasurable experience is more accessible. In other words, the more immediate and tantalizing reward dims the distant view. Very few of us, while in mortality, have seen the celestial kingdom, and we do not have a clear view of the transcendent beauty, joy, and love that will be there. We only have what the prophets tell us, such as Joseph Smith did in sections 76, 88, and 132 of the Doctrine and Covenants. The dimness of the distant view might be especially true for young people without a strong background in the gospel. As Paul teaches: "We see through the glass darkly" (1 Corinthians 13:12). Thus, that which is dimly seen reduces the incentive.

What Is the Harm in It? What about the third criteria for deciding what is right or wrong—"Where is the harm in it?" or "Aren't we doing more good than harm?" The main problem with this concept is that we do not always comprehend what the Lord sees. He understands things a lot more clearly than we do. The Lord sees things that cause us harm, which we do not see. Unfortunately, I believe this criteria is used much too frequently in the world about us, especially by young people. Let's test a few real life choices we have to make, none of which are earth shaking with regard to consequences. How about putting one quarter in a slot machine while waiting at a Las Vegas Airport? Would it have eternal consequences? Probably not. Would it do material harm to me or anyone else? Little if any. But what happens when we use the criteria, "If ye love me." If the Savior, through his servants, asks us to not gamble and if we love Him, it doesn't matter whether the amount is 25¢ or $2,500. We don't do it because the Lord has asked us not to. *When love is the criteria, size or degree becomes irrelevant.*

What is the harm in one cup of coffee? What physical harm would it do? Probably none. The spiritual impact is far more serious, because we know we would be doing something that someone we love and with whom we covenanted to obey has asked us not to do it. Also, a more long-term spiritual consequence might be our inability to answer all of the temple recommend interview questions in a positive way. But it is certainly not the most serious sin we could commit. Why would we not consider drinking a cup of coffee? If someone were to offer you one hundred dollars or a one thousand dollars to drink just one cup of coffee, using the criteria, "What harm would it do?" you would probably do it. But if your obedience is love-based, because Christ has asked you not to do so (D&C 89:9) and your love for Him is more important to you than any benefit that a monetary reward might provide, you would not do it. Perhaps it would be a real test of our love of the Savior.

How about playing with face cards? What is the long-term, eternal impact? Perhaps not much. Harm being done? Probably none. Good being done by playing with the family? Mostly good, except for the example of disobeying the prophets.[2] What about using love as the criteria? Several prophets, including Presidents Joseph F. Smith, Harold B. Lee, and Spencer W. Kimball in general conference talks advised members of the Church not to play with face cards. If we love the Lord and His servants, should we not set an example by doing what the prophets advise us to do, even if we do not understand why? Or is it okay to exhibit selective obedience? In other words, do we get to decide what part of what the prophets say is important? Does each succeeding prophet need to repeat what previous prophets have said? Why not use Rook cards and still have the benefits, without the spiritual impact? I personally believe that there will be times the Lord will test us and ask us to do things we do not understand just for the purpose of seeing if we love Him enough to obey even without understanding why. It is likely that Abraham did not understand why the Lord would ask him to offer up Isaac as a sacrifice. Did Abraham question or choose to disobey?

How about a little one-on-one basketball on Sunday afternoon or eating out at a restaurant on Sunday, where we have the option not to do so? Any harm done? The servers and cooks will already be there, but are we not making the Sabbath, a day that has been sanctified and made a holy day (Genesis 2:3), like any other day except for the time we go to church? Perhaps some good is done by being with family or friends, but are we not breaking a commandment? The Lord and his servants, the prophets, repeatedly tell us that the Sabbath has been sanctified to be a sacred day and not to engage in commercial or athletic activities. It should be reserved for spiritual growth, meditation, and spiritual service. We have been told that Saturdays and weekdays are the times for work, athletics, or fun activities.

A love of the Savior causes us to research from all of the scriptures and all of the writings of the prophets. We can learn what the Lord wants us to do on the Sabbath and then try to follow the those teachings. The other criteria for obedience do not do motivate us to do that.

There may be times when circumstances leave us no choice but to disobey a lesser law in order to obey a higher law. For example, I had a Church position in Michigan that caused me to drive to points in most of the lower peninsula of the state. My car could not make round trips on one tank of gas. I had to purchase gas on Sundays in order to fulfill church assignments. However, where there is a legitimate choice "to do" or "not to do" is where love causes us to make the only right choice.

Fear of Punishment. We do not hear a lot about punishment for sin in our church meetings. Many Christian faiths preach hell fire and damnation as a pretty fundamental doctrine that is frequently taught. Perhaps we do not do so because the Lord knows that negative motivation through fear is far less motivating than love of the Savior. However, I do not believe that we can totally ignore a fundamental doctrine of the gospel of Jesus Christ that teaches us that all who are disobedient and all who do not gain faith in Christ, repent of their sins, and be baptized will be required to endure punishment for their sins, the severity of which will be dependent upon the degree of wickedness they choose to bring into their lives. Listen to Christ speaking to the Prophet Joseph:

> For behold, I, God, have suffered these things for all, that they might not suffer if they would repent;
>
> But if they would not repent they must suffer even as I;
>
> Which suffering caused myself, even God, the greatest of all, to tremble because of pain, and to bleed at every pore, and to suffer both body and spirit—and would that I might not drink the bitter cup, and shrink—
>
> Nevertheless, glory be to the Father, and I partook and finished my preparations unto the children of men. (D&C 19:16–19)

It must be emphasized that LDS doctrine on punishment is significantly different than all other Christian faiths, in that most of them teach that punishment of the wicked will never end and all who are disobedient and fail to confess Christ will dwell with Satan and his angels in torment for eternity. In contrast, the restored gospel of Christ has revealed that there are three basic levels of disobedience or wickedness—terrestrial carnality, telestial carnality, and son of perdition carnality. All who do not implement the restored gospel of Jesus Christ into their lives will have to endure punishment for their sins; but punishment will be based upon the degree of disobedience and will end for all, except for the sons of perdition, at the time of their resurrection.

Punishment takes place during the millennium. The righteous, who fully partake of the gospel plan, will be resurrected at the time of the glorious Second Coming of the Savior and will have been sanctified and redeemed and endure no punishment. They come forth in the morning of the first resurrection. The terrestrial disobedient will have to endure a brief punishment with Satan and his angels in outer darkness and then will be resurrected onto the terrestrial earth. They come forth in the late morning or early afternoon of the first resurrection. The telestial wicked and sons of perdition endure punishment for the full thousand years of the millennia reign and then are resurrected in the final resurrection at the end of the millennium. The sons of perdition are the only ones who are required to return to dwell with Satan and his angels in eternity, after resurrection and judgment.

I believe that Latter-day Saints need to understand the ultimate plan for all of Father's children. However, we need to teach that the most motivating force that results in committed obedience is by developing a love of the Savior and not punishment.

Obedience Resulting from a Sense of Duty. While many, if not most, of us begin our initial commitment to obedience, because we feel duty bound to others (parents, spouses, or good friends), ultimately, we need to realize that a higher level of commitment results from a growing love of the Savior. However, it is better to obey due to a sense of duty than it is to be disobedient. This conclusion also applies to obedience resulting from fear or to gain an eternal reward. Obedience for any reason, except for the purpose of deception, is always a better course than disobedience, because it provides a path that can lead to a love of the Savior: "If any man will do his will, he shall know of the doctrine, whether it be of God, or whether I speak of myself" (John 7:17). Obedience for any reason can lead to a love of the Savior and a firm testimony, with one exception. Obedience for the benefit of deception indicates an evil desire and cannot result in good. Ultimately, a love of the Savior provides the highest level of commitment to obedience.

General Thoughts on Obedience

A love of the Savior as the criteria for obedience is the great leveler of all of the commandments. It makes "thou shalt not steal" almost the same as "thou shalt not put a quarter in a slot machine" and "thou shalt not bear false witness" almost the same as "thou shalt not drink one cup of coffee." Do not misunderstand. There are varying degrees of seriousness in the categories of sin that require varying degrees of punishment. But our love of the Savior makes even the little sins important to those seeking to emulate Him.

The Lord does not expect us to become perfect in one huge leap of faith. As we grow in our understanding of the Savior and His Atonement, our love for Him and testimony of Him grow and our understanding of what is required of us deepens. As these attributes grow, we also grow in our desire to be obedient and become more and more like Him, just as many of the great prophet-leaders we love live their lives. To know Him is to love Him, and to love Him creates a desire in our hearts to become like Him. The greater the love, the greater the desire.

Disobedience is an act of selfishness. Ignorance is not a factor, for when one disobeys in ignorance, there is no sin. The opposite of "If ye love me" is to say, "I don't care what you say. I am going to do what I want to do. What I want is more important to me that what you want." In a very real sense, deliberate disobedience is a rejection of the Savior. Of course, there are differing degrees of rejecting the Lord, from those who murder, rape, and pillage, to those who put a quarter in a slot machine. But one cannot say, "I love you" and then in turn say, "I don't care what you ask me to do; I'm going to do what I want."

When King Benjamin quotes to his people the words given him by an angel that "the natural man is an enemy to God, and has been from the fall of Adam, and will be forever and ever, unless he yields to the enticings of the Holy Spirit, and putteth off the natural man and becometh a saint through the Atonement of Christ" (Mosiah 3:19), he is not saying that all men are completely evil. He is just saying that, until men come to know Christ, they naturally are inclined to say, "What I want to do is more important than what He wants me to do." The natural man and the carnal, sensual, and devilish man is the antithesis of the man who loves and serves Christ. The natural man is selfish and seeks to satisfy his own pleasures, needs, and desires before anyone else. Me first, and everyone else second or third. Agency allows us to choose which level of living we desire.

Even the most righteous are not perfect but are striving to overcome the natural man and become more like the Savior. Because of our love for Heavenly Father and the Savior, we desire to pattern our lives to become like them: "What manner of men of men ought ye to be? Verily, I say unto you, even as I am" (3 Nephi 27:27). Whenever we begin to be built up because we pay our tithes, live the Word of Wisdom, attend our meetings, and render church service, we need to remember the Psalm of Nephi, and Nephi's lamentation will return to humble us (2 Nephi 4:17–19).

Every law, every commandment, and every instruction from the

Lord to the Brethren are given for the purpose of helping us become more Christlike. What was the ultimate definition of the Savior's life? He was totally submissive to the Father in every facet of His life. By loving our Father and our Savior and by living the commandments, we are on the path to becoming more Christlike. There are telestial, terrestrial, and perhaps even celestial levels of disobedience. To the degree we allow our "natural" desires to cause us to disobey is the degree in which we become and enemy to God (Mosiah 3:19).

What is it that brings about the kind of love that causes us to offer our lives unconditionally to Him and to become completely submissive? Several scriptures give us a subtle clue that answers this question. The Savior declares, "And my Father sent me that I might be lifted up upon the cross; and after that I had been lifted up upon the cross, that I might draw all men unto me" (3 Nephi 27:14; D&C 18:10–11; John 12:32). To become powerfully aware of the Savior's atoning sacrifice and His great love for us causes us to reciprocate love to the degree that it changes our lives and fills us with a desire to serve and obey Him. At that point, we no longer need to be instructed in every little detail of obedience. Then we begin to search for ways to more perfectly emulate Christ and the Father. Again I quote President Ezra Taft Benson, "When obedience ceases to be an irritant and becomes our quest, in that moment God will endow [*enable*] us with power."[3] The difference between "quest" and "irritant" is love. When we love Him, we desire to obey!

Notes

1. Ezra Taft Benson as quoted by Donald Staheli, "Obedience—Life's Great Challenge," *Ensign,* May 1998, 82.
2. Elder McConkie may disagree with some of these statements. See *Mormon Doctrine*, 1st ed., 105.
3. Ezra Taft Benson as quoted by Donald Staheli, *Ensign,* May 1998, 82.

6

Enabled to Endure

It is clear that the enabling power flowing from the Savior touches every part of our lives. That committed discipleship will require both sacrifice and adversity, as well as obedience, is also clear. The Prophet Joseph Smith, President Spencer W. Kimball, and Elder Neal A. Maxwell powerfully introduce the concepts that will be discussed in more detail in the following pages:

> Let us here observe, that a religion that does not require the sacrifice of all things never has power sufficient to produce the faith necessary unto life and salvation; for, from the first existence of man, the faith necessary unto the enjoyment of life and salvation never could be obtained without the sacrifice of all earthly things. It is through this sacrifice and this only, that God has ordained that man should enjoy eternal life; and it is through the medium of sacrifice of all earthly things that men do actually know that they are doing the things that are well pleasing in the sight of God. . . .
>
> It is in vain for persons to fancy to themselves that they are heirs with those, or can be heirs with them, who have offered their all in sacrifice unless they, in like manner, offer unto him the same sacrifice, and through that sacrifice obtain the knowledge that they are accepted of him.[1]

Is there not wisdom in his giving us trials that we might rise above them, responsibilities that we might achieve, work to harden our muscles, sorrow to try our souls? Are we not permitted temptations to

> test our strength, sickness that we might learn patience, death that we might be immortalized and glorified?
>
> But if all the sick for whom we pray were healed, if all the righteous were protected and the wicked destroyed, the whole program of the Father would be annulled and the basic principle of the gospel, free agency, would be ended. . . .
>
> If joy and peace and rewards were immediately given the doer of good, there could be no evil—all would do good, and not because of the rightness of doing good. There would be no test of strength, no development of character, no growth of power, no free agency, only satanic controls.
>
> Should all prayers be immediately answered, according to our selfish desires and our limited understanding, then there would be little or no suffering, sorrow disappointment, or even death, and if these were not, there would also be an absence of joy, success, resurrection, nor eternal life and Godhood.[2]

> If we are serious in our discipleship, Jesus will eventually request each of us to do the very things which are the most difficult for us to do. . . . Sometimes the best people have the worst experiences.[3]

> When we take Jesus' yoke upon us, this admits us eventually to what Paul called the "fellowship of [Christ's] sufferings" (Philip. 3:10). Whether illness or aloneness, injustice or rejection, etc., our comparatively small-scale sufferings, if we are meek, will sink into the very marrow of the soul. We then better appreciate, not only Jesus' suffering for us, but also His matchless character, moving us to greater adoration and even emulation.[4]

> A hundred years from now, today's seeming deprivations and tribulations will not matter then unless we let them matter too much now. A hundred years from now, today's serious physical ailment will be but a fleeting memory. . . . So much depends, therefore, upon our maintaining gospel perspective in the midst of ordinariness and the pressures of temptation, tribulation, and deprivation.[5]

The Dilemma

Perhaps there is some confusion, both in and out of the Church, as to the part that adversity plays in the scheme of things. Frequently we hear the following comments from those (or observers of those) enduring severe setbacks, losses, or burdens: "Why is the Lord punishing us (or them)?" or "What did we (they) do to deserve this?" There is a common misconception that when we are keeping the commandments, everything in our lives will be go smoothly. But you say, "Is it not true that keeping the commandments will result in blessings from Heavenly Father? Certainly, the scriptures teach that such is the case."

> Bring ye all the tithes into the storehouse, that there may be meat in my house, and prove me now herewith, saith the Lord of hosts, if I will not open you the windows of heaven, and pour you out a blessing that there shall not be room enough to contain it. (Malachi 3:10)

> There is a law irrevocably decreed in heaven before the foundation of this world, upon which all blessings are predicated—
>
> And when we obtain any blessing from God, it is by obedience to that law upon which it is predicated. (D&C 130:20–21)

It all seems pretty clear. If we keep the commandments, we'll never have problems; we'll have wealth and live long happy lives with our children growing up active in the Church, marrying in the temple, and then we'll die in our sleep after living to a goodly age. If this were the case, how would we reconcile such promises with what Joseph Smith and Spencer Kimball and Neal Maxwell teach us? Also, what about the prophets that endured such adversity and affliction. Were they being punished for some unworthiness?

Look at Joseph Smith in particular. He was continually hounded by his enemies; was charged and tried in court innumerable times on trumped up charges; had more than half of his children died before birth or before reaching maturity; had to flee Kirtland for his life, threatened by apostates and leaving most of his possessions; had to leave everything a second time in Far West, including family and friends, to be incarcerated for over six months in a filthy prison called Liberty Jail; was martyred in Carthage at the age of thirty-eight; and finally, after all this, saw (from the spirit world) most of his entire family, including his beloved Emma, leave the Church.

Look at the Savior, the person most worthy of blessings that ever lived. Look at the wealth he accumulated—"the foxes have holes, and the birds of the air have nests, but the Son of man hath not where to lay his head" (Matthew 8:20). Something must be wrong here! Are the scriptures promising blessings to the faithful mistaken? Or do we not understand them? If we understand the Lord's perspective of adversity and His desire to enable us, our understanding will help us cope with and endure when adversity and sacrifice comes our way.

Are Wealth and Prosperity Truly Blessings from God?

So strongly entrenched are the ideas that the righteous are blessed and the wicked are punished, that when we loved ones or acquaintances suffer adversity or affliction, many conclude that something is wrong or that we are being punished. Again the answer seems clear from the scriptures. Look at the ageless Nephite cycles in the Book of Mormon. There are countless times where, as the people become righteous, they are blessed; they become prosperous; prosperity brings pride and wickedness; they are subjected to wars, sickness, disease, and tribulation until they turn righteous again; then the cycle starts over again. Was it not wealth and prosperity that brought the people into wickedness? Does it make sense that God's blessings would be things that produce pride, willfulness, and unrighteousness among so many?

Could it be that the wealth and prosperity were not really the blessings flowing from their righteousness? Might it be that their righteousness caused them to be industrious, hard working, and unified in their efforts to the point that the wealth and prosperity resulted? Perhaps wealth and prosperity were offshoots of their righteous condition, not direct blessings from God. If you question that wealth and prosperity were not the powerful causes of pride and wickedness, read Mormon's editorial comments in Helaman 3:36, 4:12, 12:2, and 13:21.

Elder Marion D. Hanks taught that when the Nephites were promised they would "prosper in the land" if they kept the commandments, it did not necessarily mean in relation to physical possessions. He used 2 Nephi 1:20 to conclude that prosperity meant "to be in the constant influence of the Lord's presence." Which would we rather have, wealth, or what Nephi was promised—the presence of the Lord?

"Inasmuch as ye shall keep my commandments ye shall prosper in the land; but inasmuch as ye will not keep my commandments ye shall be cut off from my presence."

President Brigham Young clearly states: "When I see this people grow and spread and prosper, I feel there is more danger than when they are in poverty. Being driven from city to city or into the mountains is nothing compared to the danger of our becoming rich and being hailed by outsiders as a first-class community."[6]

Did President Young see our day? Are we not prosperous and wealthy in comparison with all other times and all other areas of the world? Are we not being hailed as first-class citizens? Have we need to fear? Have Latter-day Saints become so enamored with Babylon they see wealth and prosperity as the desired blessings of God? Could it be that the blessings we sometime seek—wealth and prosperity—might be the most difficult of all the trials or tests that might be placed upon us? Could it be that having "sufficient for our needs" might be a better immediate goal, and having "all things in common" with "no rich and no poor among us" the ideal? It should be noted that there are many Latter-day Saints who have wealth and maintain proper perspective while enduring this trial. But it is not easy. There were few periods in Nephite history where they were able to endure—the two hundred year period after the Savior's personal ministry among them being the most significant exception. After two hundred years, prosperity began to take its toll.

The Savior cautioned, "Verily, I say unto you, that a rich man shall hardly enter into the kingdom of heaven. And again I say unto you, It is easier for a camel to go through the eye of a needle, than for a rich man to enter into the kingdom of God" (Matthew 19:23–24). Maybe the Lord didn't really mean what He said? Surely something that seems so desirable can't be that bad. It is interesting to read all that the Lord has said in the scriptures and through modern prophets with regard to wealth. But that is beyond the scope of this chapter. We can take at face value that the Savior knew what He was talking about. Perhaps most of the profound and lasting blessings promised the faithful are not of this world. "For whoso is faithful . . . receiveth my Father's Kingdom; therefore all that my Father hath shall be given to him" (D&C 84:33–38).

What is required for us to achieve such profound blessings as "all that my Father hath"? Remember what Joseph Smith told us in his statement at the beginning of this chapter: "Let us here observe, that a religion that does not require the sacrifice of all things never has power sufficient to produce the faith necessary unto life and salvation." Our willingness to sacrifice "all things," a quality enhanced by the enabling power of the Savior, is perhaps a key element to receive that blessing.

One need only consider the sacrifice required of Abraham in his willingness to offer his most beloved son, Isaac, to really understand the full significance of the preceding statement. Then we must ask, "How can a person be tested on his ability to sacrifice 'all things' without tests, trials, and adversities?" Do the righteous sometimes seem to suffer pain, sorrow, death, loss of jobs, business failures, and the loss of loved ones more than seems to be just? Does it sometimes seem that the blatantly wicked and disobedient (movie stars, ruthless industry leaders, and so forth) seem to have "everything"? Is it possible that some of the most significant rewards, and punishments for that matter, for our activities in this life come at a later time? This is what President Kimball told us at the beginning of this chapter.

Spiritual Strength from Adversity

Again, as persecution escalated in Far West, the Prophet was asked why the Lord allowed the Saints to endure such hardships. Remember that many of them had already fled Kirtland to escape apostate vengeance and then shortly thereafter had been driven out of Jackson County; leaving homes, businesses, and most of their belongings a second time because of mob violence. After some thought, the Prophet answered with a scripture: "Therefore let you hearts be comforted; for all things shall work together for good to them that walk uprightly, and to the sanctification of the church. For I will raise up unto me a pure people, that will serve me in righteousness" (D&C 100:15–16).

Basically, Joseph's answer told the Saints that their adversities would purify them and refine them into a people the Lord wanted them to be. Ore containing precious metals such as gold and silver is refined in a smelter, furnace, or a refinery. The ore is melted and the difference in density and burning point in the various components allow the impurities to either burn off or float to the top of the molten mass. The precious metals, after the refining process, are pure and possess a beauty that they did not previously have. Can men be refined and purified from the impurities they possess?

> And he shall sit as a refiner and purifier of silver: and he shall purify the sons of Levi, and purge them as gold and silver, that they may offer unto the Lord an offering in righteousness. (Malachi 3:3)

> And it shall come to pass, that in all the land, saith the Lord, two parts therein shall be cut off and die; but the third shall be left therein.
>
> And I will bring the third part through the fire, and will refine them as silver is refined, and will try them as gold is tried; they shall call on my name, and I will hear them: I will say, It is my people: and they shall say, The Lord is my God. (Zechariah 13:8–9)

What is the refiner's fire? Certainly for the Saints in the early days of the Church, it was easy to see the refining process as the trials, adversities, and persecutions they endured. Perhaps our adversity is wealth and prosperity which, according to Brigham Young, is much more deadly. What we do with that which is given us may be the test. For most Saints the payment of a tithe and a five-dollar fast offering probably just isn't going to cut it in order to stand with the early Saints and say, "We paid the same price you did."

It is clear that adversity and suffering perfects the soul, although it is true that these experiences can also condemn us, if we rebel against God because of the adversity. It depends on how we handle that which is dealt to us. Even the Savior's perfectness came by trial and suffering: "Though he were a Son, yet learned he obedience by the things which he suffered; and being made perfect he became the author of eternal salvation unto all them that obey him" (Hebrews 5:8–9).

If Christ could not learn obedience and become perfect except through suffering and adversity, how much more would we need the same refinement, only to a much higher degree? King Benjamin, in quoting the words of the angel, indicates that our lives must endure affliction: "For the natural man is an enemy to God, and has been from the fall of Adam, and will be forever and ever, unless he yields to the enticings of the Holy Spirit, and putteth off the natural man and becometh a saint through the Atonement of Christ the Lord, and becometh as a child, submissive, meek, humble, patient, full of love, willing to submit to all things which the Lord seeth fit to inflict upon him" (Mosiah 3:19).

According to the angel, who (we have to assume) had access to a pretty good source, the natural man has to be refined to the position of a saint by the things inflicted upon him by the Lord. This sainthood also has to be in conjunction with the Atonement of the Savior and what the Holy Ghost does in producing a "mighty change" in our hearts.

Does the Lord take pleasure in inflicting His children? No! He sees it as the only way to refine us to be the kind of people He needs us to be. Both Solomon and Paul go so far as to say that if we do not have adversity in our lives, we probably have need to worry:

> And ye have forgotten the exhortation which speaketh unto you as unto children, My son, despise not thou the chastening of the Lord, nor faint when thou art rebuked of him:
>
> For whom the Lord loveth he chasteneth, and scourgeth every son whom he receiveth.
>
> If ye endure chastening, God dealeth with you as with sons; for what son is he whom the father chasteneth not?
>
> But if ye be without chastisement, whereof all are partakers, then ye are bastards [illegitimate and not heirs], and not sons. (Hebrews 12:5–8)

Those who have determined to serve the Lord at all costs will not be without their afflictions to test their resolve and to purify their souls. I have seen it happen many times: a person reaches the point of committing himself totally to the Lord, then the tests and trials begin. President Kimball and Elder Maxwell concur with this conclusion, as shown by their comments at the beginning of this chapter. The Lord, in answering Joseph's prayerful plea for understanding from the foul dungeon of Liberty Jail in Missouri, told us the purpose of affliction. Listen to the Lord's answer to Joseph Smith:

> My son, peace be unto thy soul; thine adversity and thine afflictions shall be but a small moment; and then, if thou endure it well, God shall exalt thee on high; thou shalt triumph over all thy foes. (D&C 121:7–8)

> And if thou shouldst be cast into the pit, or into the hands of murderers, and the sentence of death passed upon thee; if thou be cast into the deep; if the billowing surge conspire against thee; if fierce winds become thine enemy; if the heavens gather blackness, and all the elements combine to hedge up the way; and above all, if the very jaws of hell shall gape open the mouth wide after thee, know thou, my son, that all these things shall give thee experience, and shall be for thy good.
>
> The Son of Man hath descended below them all. Art thou greater than he? Therefore . . . fear not what man can do, for God shall be with you forever and ever. (D&C 122:7–9)

Experiencing adversity and tribulation is a necessary part of our mortal experience and will be for our ultimate good.

What the Prophets Have Said

The comments of the prophets on the necessity of trial and adversity are so voluminous it would fill a book. Each contributes their own perspective on its purpose and the part it plays in preparing us for our eternal destiny. First, remember President Kimball's "Tragedy or Destiny" talk given at the BYU devotional mentioned at the beginning of this chapter. Now listen to Elder Orson F. Whitney, whom President Kimball quoted:

> No pain that we suffer, nor trial that we experience is wasted. It ministers to our education, to the development of such qualities as patience, faith, fortitude, and humility. All that we suffer and all that we endure, especially when we endure it patiently, builds up our characters, purifies our hearts, expands our souls, and makes us more tender and charitable, more worthy to be called the children of God . . . and it

is through sorrow and suffering, toil and tribulation, that we gain the education that we come here to acquire and which will make us more like our Father and Mother in heaven.[7]

President Kimball then went on to say in his "Tragedy Or Destiny" message, that if he had unlimited priesthood power with the limited vision he had (for we "see through the glass darkly" as Paul said), he may have saved Abinadi from being burned at the stake, and thus, prevented him from receiving a martyr's reward. He also may have warded off the Savior's suffering in the garden and on the cruel cross; healed Paul of his affliction; destroyed the mob at Carthage jail; and certainly never let loved ones or friends suffer pain or death. Then he asked the question, "Would such acts have been in harmony with God's will?"

During the height of the persecution of the saints in Far West, Missouri (March 25, 1839), the Prophet Joseph Smith sent an epistle from Liberty Jail to members of the Church containing numerous precious gems of doctrine. Included was the following counsel in relation to their persecutions:

> And now, beloved brethren, we say unto you, that inasmuch as God hath said that He would have a tried people, that He would purge them as gold, now we think that this time He has chosen to be His own crucible, wherein we have been tried; and we think if we get through with any degree of safety, and shall have kept the faith, that it will be a sign to this generation, altogether sufficient to leave them without excuse; and we think also, it will be a trial of our faith equal to that of Abraham, and that the ancients will not have whereof to boast over us in the day of judgment, as being called to pass through heavier afflictions; that we may hold an even weight in the balance with them; but now, after having suffered so great sacrifice and having passed through so great a season of sorrow, we trust that a ram may be caught in the thicket speedily, to relieve the sons and daughters of Abraham from their great anxiety, and to light up the lamp of salvation upon their countenances, that they may hold on now, after having gone so far unto everlasting life.[8]
>
> It is a shame to the Saints to talk of chastisements, and transgressions, when all the Saints before them, [even] prophets and apostles,

have had to come up through great tribulation; whether a Herod, a Nero, or a Boggs, causes the affliction, or the blood to be shed, is all the same—these murderers will have their reward! and the saints theirs.[9]

President Young knew well the harsh hand of adversity and trial and spoke of it:

> The people of the Most High God must be tried. It is written that they will be tried in all things, even as Abraham was tried. If we are called to go upon mount Moriah to sacrifice a few of our Isaacs, it is no matter; we may just as well do that as anything else. I think there is a prospect for the Saints to have all the trials they wish for, or can desire. . . . Every calamity that can come upon mortal beings will be suffered to come upon the few, to prepare them to enjoy the presence of the Lord. If we obtain the glory that Abraham obtained, we must do so by the same means that he did.[10]

> Now if you possess the light of the Holy Spirit, you can see clearly that trials in the flesh are actually necessary.[11]

> Let any people enjoy peace and quiet, unmolested, undisturbed—never be persecuted for their religion, and they are very likely to neglect their duty, to become cold and indifferent, and lose their faith.
>
> The Lord has his design in this. You may ask what his design is. You all know that the Saints must be made pure, to enter into the celestial kingdom. It is recorded that Jesus was made perfect through suffering. . . . Why should we imagine for one moment that we can be prepared to enter into the kingdom of rest with him and the Father, without passing through similar ordeals?[12]

Also John Taylor was hardly a stranger to trial as he spoke on the subject:

> I heard the Prophet Joseph say, in speaking to the Twelve on one occasion: "You will have all kinds of trials to pass through. And it is quite as necessary for you to be tried as it was for Abraham and other men of God, and (said he) God will feel after you, and He will take hold of you and wrench your very heart strings, and if you cannot stand it you will not be fit for an inheritance in the Celestial Kingdom of God."[13]

Then President Lorenzo Snow offered this insight:

> For everything you have suffered, for everything that has occurred to you which you thought evil at the time, you will receive four fold, and that suffering will have had a tendency to make you better and stronger and to feel that you have been blessed. When you look back over your experiences you will see that you have advanced far ahead and have gone up several rounds of the ladder toward exaltation and glory.[14]

Finally, the Prophet Joseph stated with regard to those who would be worthy to receive the Second Comforter—those receiving the personal ministration of the Savior while yet in mortality: "When the Lord has thoroughly proved him, and finds that the man is determined to serve Him at all hazards, then the man will find his calling and his election made sure, then it will be his privilege to receive the other Comforter, which the Lord hath promised the Saints."[15]

How can we "be proven and determined to serve Him at all hazards" if there are no trials or adversities in our lives? Is it not clear from what the apostles and prophets have said, that adversity in the end will be a great blessing in our lives? Will it not help us to become the type of people the Lord desires us to be?

Should We Seek Adversity and Trial?

It is also clear from what the prophets have said that we should not seek out adversity and trial.

> I do not desire trials; I do not desire affliction. I would pray to God to "leave me not in temptation, and deliver me from evil; for thine is the kingdom, the power, and the glory." But if the earthquake bellows, the lightenings flash, the thunders roll, and the powers of darkness are let loose, and the spirit of evil is permitted to rage, and an evil influence is brought to bear on the Saints, and my life, with theirs is put to the test; let it come, for we are the Saints of the most High God, and all is well, all is peace, all is right, and will be both in time and eternity. . . .
>
> But I do not want trials.[16]

In fact, as President Taylor suggests, it is not inappropriate to pray for relief and seek measures from which relief can come. But until we are delivered, we should never be among those who "curse God and die," but understand the purpose of that which we endure and "endure it well." Knowing that trial and adversity are necessary for our good changes our perspective, helps to eliminate the depression, causes us to turn to Father who will sustain us during our affliction, and gives us strength through the love we have for Him and the Savior.

Always remember that adversity does not mean God has forsaken us. Instead, He has given us an exercise to strengthen us and change us into the kind of person He wants us to be. Also remember that He has promised to help us during trials and that they will never be beyond our strength to endure. Read Paul's promise: "There hath no temptation taken you but such as is common to man: but God is faithful, who will not suffer you to be tempted [or tried] above that ye are able; but will with the temptation [or trial] also make a way to escape, that ye may be able to bear it" (1 Corinthians 10:13).

Instead of turning from prayer when adversity comes which is what the adversary wants us to do, it should turn us to more intense prayer with fasting and increased commitment and obedience. Prayer and exercising faith are the secret ingredients that turn adversity into spiritual muscles through the enabling power of Christ.

Adversity Is Sometimes Used to Change Our Direction

Sometimes we choose to set out on a course contrary to the plan of our Heavenly Father. He knows the direction that best defines our true destiny, even though our course may be a worthy effort. Some things we experience in life that we look upon as an affliction, may be true blessings in disguise.

President Hugh B. Brown eloquently tells of how the direction of his life was changed by the Lord. First, he speaks of an experience he had as a young gardener with a currant bush. The bush had grown huge, almost to treelike proportions. Knowing that such bushes use so much energy to produce limbs and branches, he determined to prune it back so that it could produce fruit. After the pruning, there was little left but stumps and roots.

Tenderly he considered what was left. The currant bush looked so sad and deeply hurt. On every stump there seemed to be a tear where the pruning knife had cut away the growth of early spring. The poor bush seemed to speak to him, and he thought he heard it say: "Oh how could you be so cruel to me; you who claim to be my friend, who planted me and cared for me when I was young, and nurtured and encouraged me to grow? Could you not see that I was rapidly responding to your care? I was nearly half as large as the trees across the fence and might soon have become like one of them. But now you've cut my branches back; the green, attractive leaves are gone, and I am in disgrace among my fellows."

The young gardener looked at the current bush and heard its plea with sympathy and understanding. His voice was full of kindness as he replied:

> I am the gardener here. Do not cry; what I have done to you was necessary that you might be a prize currant bush in my garden. You were not intended to give shade or shelter by your branches. My purpose when I planted you was that you should bear fruit. When I want currants, a tree, regardless of its size, cannot supply the need.
>
> So my little current bush, if I had allowed you to continue to grow as you had started, all your strength would have gone to wood, your roots would not have gained a firm hold, and the purpose for which I brought you into my garden would have been defeated; your place would have been taken by another for you would have been barren. You must not weep; all this will be for your good, and some day, when you see more clearly, when you are richly laden with luscious fruit, you will thank me and say, "Surely he was a wise and loving gardener. He knew the purpose for my being, and I thank him now for what I then thought was cruelty."

Some years later, this young gardener was in a foreign land, and he, himself, was growing. He had achieved the rank of colonel in the Canadian army and was proud of his position and ambitions for the future. One day an unexpected vacancy as a brigadier general opened, and President Brown was directly in line for the position. The goal to which he had aspired was almost within his grasp. But for some reason, unknown to him at the time, the promotion was given to another, a less qualified person, or so he thought. He was asked to take another relatively unimportant post, which, under the circumstances, caused his friends to feel that he had failed. He staggered to his tent and knelt beside his cot and wept. He knew now that he could never hope to have what he had thought was so desirable.

He cried to God and said: "Oh how could you have been so cruel to me? You who claim to be my friend; you who brought me here and nurtured and encouraged me to grow. Could you not see that I was almost equal to the other men whom I have so long admired? But now I have been cut down. I am in disgrace among my fellows. Oh, how could you do this to me?"

President Brown was humiliated and chagrined, and even had a drop of bitterness in his heart, as he states. As he knelt and wept he seemed to hear an echo from the past. Where had he heard those words before? They seemed familiar: "I am the gardener here." He caught his breath. Ah, that was it—the currant bush! Why should that long forgotten incident come to him in the midst of his hour of tragedy? And then memory answered with words he himself had spoken: "Do not cry. . . . What I have done to you was necessary. . . . You were not intended for what you sought to be. . . . If I had allowed you to continue . . . you would have failed in your purpose for which I planted you and my plans for you would have been defeated. You must not weep; some day when you are richly laden with experience you will say, 'He was a wise gardener. He knew the purpose of my earth life. . . . I thank him now for what I thought was so cruel.' "

There was no bitterness in his heart as he humbly spoke again to God and said, "I know you now. You are the gardener, and I the currant bush. Help me, dear God, to endure the pruning, and to grow as you would have me grow; to take my allotted place in life and ever more to say, 'Thy will be done.' "

President Brown's own words were the medium by which his prayer was answered. Had he succeeded in becoming a general in the Canadian army, we may never have heard this talk given at general conference by a member of the First Presidency of the Church. What happened to President Brown, is likely not an uncommon occurrence among the those committed to follow Christ.[17]

Source of Adversity

Now that we have a clear understanding of the Lord's perspective of adversity from the scriptures and the prophets and the fact that at times we are the current bush and the Lord is the Gardner, what does this mean to us here and now? First, it is clear that all adversity is not the same for everyone. In some instances we bring adversity on ourselves. An example might be those who break the Word of Wisdom. Some are likely to suffer the consequences of their own choices or the choices of others, such as accidents related to alcohol abuse that take lives; deadly or debilitating diseases or physical ailments from the use of tobacco; or spouses who choose to break their covenants to the Lord, leaving single-parent families to cope with survival.

On the other hand, the Lord provides some adversities that are specifically designed for us to help us become what the Lord wants us to become; for example, the responsibility of raising children born with severe physical ailments that need extensive nurturing and physical care; the early loss of a spouse before children are raised; accidents that take lives the lives of loved ones; repeated business failures that might come to keep us humble or avoid having to endure one of the hardest all the trials that could be placed upon us–wealth and affluence. Then for some of us our adversity will be to have wealth and affluence. Wealth is perhaps one of the hardest of all tests; a test to see if we can meet that challenge in the way the Lord wants us to do so. Although, at the time, it seems to be the nicest to have and easiest to bear.

Then perhaps there are those who do not need a lot of adversity to become what the Lord wants them to become. The Lord told Joseph Smith that little children who die in their infancy were so tender and pure, they did not have to endure the trials of this earth to be worthy of the celestial kingdom. But my understanding of what the prophets have said is that most of us who have committed to serve the Lord will have to endure trial and adversity in our lives in order to develop the qualities of character the Lord wants us to have. It may be early in our lives or it may come later, but it will likely come. Why adversities for some seem to be more severe than others, I do not know. But the Lord knows and someday we will know as well.

Our Response to Adversity

What are we to do when severe adversities and trials come into our lives? In such situations we sometimes do not even feel like praying, studying the scriptures, serving others, and so forth. Depression is a force that seems to keep us from doing that which will bring relief to our souls. Not too long after the Prophet Joseph had asked the members of the Church to go to Missouri to begin to build the center stake of Zion in Jackson County, they began to suffer great persecution and began to murmur and complain. The Lord told them to "be still and know that I am God" (D&C 101:16).

That is the first thing we have to do. Go to the temple, a hilltop, or to another quiet, secluded place. Know that Father is there; know that He loves you; know that there is a reason for these things happening over which you have no control; and know that through Him peace can come into your soul even while you are in the midst of tribulation. Draw upon your love for God and for the Savior, whom you have come to love because you have felt His love for you in the suffering He endured. While in the Garden of Gethsemane, the Savior cried in agony to the Father, "Abba, Father, all things are possible unto thee; take away this cup from me: nevertheless not what I will, but what thou wilt" (Mark 14:36). As a result of his request, an angel was sent to help Him endure his suffering (Luke 22:43). But remember, the cup was not taken away until He became aware that the price had been paid. Then He allowed peace to come when He said, "It is finished," and allowed His spirit to leave His suffering body.

Remember as a member of the Church, having the Holy Ghost, Christ has promised to give you peace: "Peace I leave with you, my peace I give unto you: not as the world giveth, give I unto you. Let not your heart be troubled, neither let it be afraid" (John 14:17).

Do you believe that your Savior will keep his promise to you? I do! However, there is a price to be paid in the effort you make in prayer; in "being still" and knowing that He is God; in pondering and internalizing the scriptures; and in a covenant-type commitment to be obedient. Let me emphasize "be still." Listen, each time you pray and ponder and covenant. It may take days, weeks, or even longer. Remember that it took Enos "all day into the night." But maybe the Lord was requiring more of him than He will of you.

What will you be after your experience? You will be more committed. Spiritual muscles will have been developed that you did not notice before. Peace will be your friend and you will have come to know the Savior much more personally. As you look back, you may say it was well worth the experience for the blessing obtained, just as did a participant of the Martin Handcart Company that was stranded by the early winter blizzard in Wyoming during their long trek out to the desert valley of the Great Salt Lake. Many years later, this is what he said in a Sunday School class to those that were criticizing the leadership who authorized the late start:

> I ask you to stop this criticism. You are discussing a matter you know nothing about. Cold historic facts . . . give no proper interpretation of the questions involved. Mistake to send the Handcart Company out so late in the season? Yes. But I was in that company and my wife . . . too. We suffered beyond anything you can imagine and many died of exposure and starvation, but . . . we became acquainted with [God] in our extremities.
>
> I have pulled my handcart when I was so weak and weary from illness and lack of food that I could hardly put one foot ahead of the other. I have looked ahead and I seen a patch of sand or a hill slope and have said, "I can go that far and there I must give up, for I cannot pull the load through it." I have gone on to that sand and when I reached it, the cart began pushing me. I have looked back many times to see who was pushing my cart, but my eyes saw no one. I knew that the angels of God were there.
>
> Was I sorry that I chose to come by handcart? No! Neither then nor any minute of my life since. *The price we paid to become acquainted with God was a privilege to pay, and I am thankful that I was privileged to come in the Martin Handcart Company.*[18]

Would that wonderfully good, pioneer brother want to endure the trial again? Probably not, but from hindsight he saw the experience as a great blessing in his life. From hindsight your adversities will become blessings, if you meet them with faith and overcome them! Remember to keep locked in your heart a knowledge of the enabling powers that flow to us from Christ. The Father will never require of us adversity, or trial or sacrifice that is beyond our strength to endure. Through our love for Him and our knowledge of His suffering for us, we will be able to withstand the refiners fire that will ultimately purify us and seal us His.

NOTES

1. N. B. Lundwall, Comp., *Lectures on Faith* (Salt Lake City: Bookcraft, n.d.).
2. Spencer W. Kimball, "Tragedy or Destiny," BYU Devotional, Dec. 6, 1955.
3. Neal A. Maxwell, in *Church News*, Aug. 10, 2002, 5.
4. Neal A. Maxwell, " 'From Whom All Blessings Flow,' " *Ensign,* May 1997, 12.
5. Neal A. Maxwell, "Grounded, Rooted, Established, and Settled," *BYU Speeches 1981–82,* 19.
6. Brigham Young, *Journal of Discourses,* 12:272.
7. Spencer W. Kimball, "Tragedy or Destiny," BYU Devotional.
8. Joseph Smith, *Teachings of the Prophet Joseph Smith,* 135–36.
9. Ibid., 261.
10. Brigham Young, *Discourses of Brigham Young,* comp. John A. Widtsoe (Salt Lake City: Deseret Book, 1925), 529.
11. Ibid., 530–31.
12. Ibid., 531.
13. John Taylor, *Journal of Discourses,* 24:197.
14. Lorenzo Snow, *Teachings of Lorenzo Snow,* 117.
15. Joseph Smith, *Teachings of the Prophet Joseph Smith,* 150.
16. John Taylor, *Journal of Discourses,* 5:115–16.
17. Hugh B. Brown, *Eternal Quest* (Bookcraft 1956), 241–46.
18. David O. McKay, *Relief Society Magazine,* Jan. 1948, 8, quoted by Robert L. Backman, "Faith in Every Footstep," *Ensign,* Jan. 1997, 7–8; emphasis added.

Appendix

Synonymous Terms Relating to Born of the Spirit

A mighty change in your heart (Alma 5:12–14; Mosiah 5:2)
Baptized with fire and the Holy Ghost (3 Nephi 9:20; John 1:33; Matthew 3:11)
Birth of or born of the Spirit (Mosiah 17:24)
Born again (Mosiah 27:25; Moses 6:59)
Born of God (Alma 36:5; 5:14; Mosiah 27:25)
Born of the Holy Ghost (D&C 5:16)
Conversion/converted (Luke 22:32)
First Comforter (John 14:26)
Gift of the Holy Ghost (Articles of Faith 1:4)
New creatures of the Holy Ghost (Mosiah 27:26)
Receive the Holy Ghost (John 20:22; 2 Nephi 31:13)
Redeemed of the Lord (Mosiah 27:24)
Remission of sin by fire and the Holy Ghost (2 Nephi 31:17)
Sanctified by the Spirit (Alma 13:12; 5:54; Moroni 10:33)

Terms Related to Born of the Spirit

Broken Heart and Contrite Spirit: The primary offering, resulting from deep heartfelt repentance and from faith in and love for the Lord Jesus Christ, that is required to obtain the rebirth (2 Nephi 2:6–7; 3 Nephi 9:20).

Calling and Election: After one has built upon his continuing experiences with the rebirth, endured the heat of the day, and has been tested and tried in all things and proven faithful, the Lord will confirm to that person by the Spirit through personal revelation that his name is written in the Lamb's Book of Life never to be removed (D&C 131:5).

Carnality of Man: The condition of all men, in varying degrees, who have not partaken of the Atonement and gift of the Holy Ghost. There are differing degrees of carnality, from terrestrial carnality to the sons of perdition (Mosiah 3:19, 16:1–5; Alma 41:11–13, 26:21, 42:10–14; Ether 3:2; D&C 20:20; Moses 5:13 and 55, 6:15 and 49).

Cleansed by Christ: The initial and continuing cleansing that frees one from previous sin so that the Holy Ghost can come into us, sanctify us, and baptize us with fire (Moses 6:59).

Confirmation or Laying on of Hands: The ordinance that confers the right to receive the Holy Ghost (Articles of Faith 1:4).

Forgiveness: One blessing that comes with rebirth. A person must become aware of his condition in relations to the suffering of Jesus Christ to be able to offer a broken heart and a contrite spirit. It begins with awareness of a person's own unworthiness and desperate need for the Atonement of Jesus Christ (2 Nephi 31:17; Alma 36:19).

Gifts of the Spirit: The spiritual blessing that comes freely to those whose skirts are cleansed by the blood of Christ and who are sanctified by the Spirit (1 Corinthians 12; Moroni 10; D&C 46). See Bruce R. McConkie, "Gifts of the Spirit," *Mormon Doctrine,* (Salt Lake City: Bookcraft, 1951), 228.

More Sure Word of Prophecy: Synonymous with Calling and Election, which means that a man is sealed up to eternal life (D&C 131:5).

Second Comforter: Joseph Smith stated that after a person's calling and election is made sure and he strives with all his heart to draw close to the Savior, the Lord Jesus Christ will establish direct communion with that person, as John describes in the Book of Revelation: "Behold I stand at the door, and knock: if any man hear my voice, and open the door, I will come in to him, and will sup with him, and he with me" (Revelation 3:20). I personally believe that this experience is what gave Enoch and many of the Prophets the power they had: "And so great was the faith of Enoch that he led the people of God . . . and he spake the word of the Lord, and the earth trembled, and the mountains fled, even according to his command; and the rivers of water were turned out of their course . . . and all nations feared greatly, so powerful was the word of Enoch, and so great was the power of the language which God had given him" (Moses 7:13). The fact that the Savior, as Jehovah, invited the entire nation of Israel to come before Him and commune with Him, seems to indicate that He wanted them to know that He was available to them, even though I'm sure He knew that they were unworthy and unable to come into His presence (Exodus 19:3–6; D&C 84:19–24).

Sons and Daughters of Christ: The name by which we are called and the relationship we achieve through the rebirth process (Mosiah 5:7).

Testimony/Witness of the Spirit: A preliminary experience available from the Holy Ghost to both members and non-members that testifies or witnesses to truth. A visitation (temporary to non-members) by the Holy Ghost providing a witness or testimony to one seeking to know what is true (Moroni 10:4).

Water Baptism: Baptism by one having authority is the signing of a spiritual contract, wherein we agree to exercise faith in Jesus Christ and repent of our sins, and the Savior agrees to redeem and sanctify us, so we will be able to enter into His rest (2 Nephi 31).

E. Richard Packham

E. Richard Packham grew up in the little farming community of Burley, Idaho, during the depression years. He is currently married to his wonderful companion of many years, Beverly Packham. They have nine children, consisting of six sons and three daughters. Seven of their children have served missions for the Church.

Richard worked his way through several years of college earning a BS degree in chemical engineering from the University of Idaho and an MBA Degree from Northwestern University in Chicago, Illinois.

Richard spent about half his working years as an engineer and the remainder in executive positions in large regional bank leasing subsidiaries and smaller corporations.

His Church service includes serving as a missionary to the Great Lakes Mission, the bishop of the Saginaw-Midland Ward (Midland), the first counselor in the Lansing Michigan Stake presidency, and the stake president of the Mid-Michigan Stake. Richard was ordained a patriarch while working in Montgomery, Alabama. Richard and his wife served as CES missionaries on the Sioux Indian Reservation in Pine Ridge, South Dakota. They also served as ordinance workers for a number of years in the Salt Lake and the Orlando Florida Temples.

Beverly and Richard are currently enjoying retirement and living in Mesa, Arizona.

0 26575 52279 2